The practical approach to skills analysis

Other titles in the McGraw-Hill European series in
Management and Marketing

The practical approach to skills analysis

Edwin J. Singer and John Ramsden

Senior Partner   *Partner*

Urwick, Orr & Partners Limited

McGRAW-HILL · LONDON

New York · Sydney · Toronto · Mexico · Johannesburg · Panama

Published by

McGRAW-HILL Publishing Company Limited

MAIDENHEAD · BERKSHIRE · ENGLAND

07 094211 0

PRINTED AND BOUND IN GREAT BRITAIN

To **W. Douglas Seymour**
who first thought of it all

Contents

Acknowledgements

Skills analysis has now become so much a part of the training vocabulary that we are inclined to forget that this approach to identify the real skills possessed by operators, as a basis for designing training programmes, is only a quarter of a century old. One of the advantages of rapid implementation of technological change and the use of new ideas is that the authors of those ideas have a reasonable chance of seeing the fulfilment of a dream come true in their lifetime. Fortunately, this has happened to W. Douglas Seymour, who, with his brother A. H. Seymour, first thought up the 'new' approach to the problems of shop-floor learning. It is impossible to quantify the debt which the authors owe to this man. Over fifteen years, he has trained one of them and always been ready and willing to give unstintingly of his help, advice, experience, and time. Hence the dedication.

A book, based largely on case study experience, owes most of its content to others. First, we wish to acknowledge the help and encouragement given by our colleagues in Urwick, Orr & Partners, particularly to Mrs A. L. T. Taylor who has contributed so much to our thinking. Second, we express our thanks to Mr L. D. Cowan of the Perkins Engine Company who has painstakingly read the script as it emerged and made so many helpful suggestions. Third, we acknowledge a great debt to Mr V. Hampson-Jones, of the Department of Extra-Mural Studies of the University College of South Wales and Monmouthshire, who not only read and commented on the script as an act of friendship, but also drew our attention to St Thomas Aquinas, one of the foremost 'schoolmen' of the thirteenth century. Finally, there are those countless men and women in industry and commerce, managers and operators, supervisors, and craftsmen, young and old, without whom none of this would have been worthwhile doing or, indeed, possible.

Edwin J. Singer
John Ramsden

Foreword

by
T. H. R. PERKINS
Managing Director, Perkins Engines Ltd.

If managers could determine their requirements for labour in the ideal industrial situation, training would largely be unnecessary. Industry would recruit employees capable of meeting in full the requirements of their jobs from the moment they joined an organization, and able quickly to adapt their skills and knowledge to changing technological requirements and operating needs. Unfortunately, this idyllic situation does not exist. We have to accept that few, if any, employees enter our factories and offices able to meet our requirements without some familiarization, and employees have to acquire many of the skills and much of the knowledge we require of them after they have joined the company. We have to incur the considerable overhead expenditure involved in training, whether it be the hidden costs of learning informally, or the direct costs of providing controlled and organized training.

Although these overheads are accepted as inevitable, every manager must endeavour to control and reduce them. Important though they are, costs are not the only consideration. Training demands capital equipment, qualified manpower in the form of instructors and training officers, and space that could perhaps be used for manufacturing or to provide facilities for other functions. All of these can be in short supply, and a management decision may have to be made on the priority with which these resources can be allocated to the various demands for them within an organization. If training is merely an activity carried out for social, rather than profit orientated motives, it is likely to fare badly when the demand for such resources exceeds the supply.

This book deals with profitable training. Its theme is that properly organized and controlled training has a significant contribution to make in reducing the operating costs of any company. The authors set out to show line management how to make non-supervisory training effective, and how training costs can be more than offset by resultant improvements in operating efficiency. They explain the nature of training costs and provide a guide to the techniques that have been successful in making training effective in a large number of companies.

Many managers have difficulty in accepting that the techniques proven in other companies are applicable in the particular circumstances of their own organization. By drawing on their considerable experience as management consultants specializing in training, the authors have been able to illustrate the points they make with examples and case studies from a wide range of companies and industries. As a result they are able to demonstrate that specific results have been obtained from general principles capable of broad application.

The general application of these principles would undoubtedly result in improved utilization of manpower and more profitable business.

Part I

1. Introduction

A frequent complaint levelled against line managers is that they fail to recognize the importance of the work of training staffs in industry and commerce. Training staffs often consider themselves underpaid, their enthusiasm unrewarded, and their status within their companies not commensurate with their importance and value. It is a common occurrence for a training officer to produce a first-class manual which would reduce greatly the period of training, only to find that managers evince little interest in it, and even less readiness to implement its recommendations in practical training. A major cause of this situation is the failure of the training staff themselves, perhaps in some cases due to their own lack of ability or confidence, to convince managers of the utility of their work. There exists a 'chicken and egg' situation in which forceful, competent men are often unwilling to enter the training field because they think that its importance is considered low by most managements. Thus, the training staff appointed often are not the type of people who are able to command the attention of managers. Those who enter 'training' often remain a few years in the function and then move on to other fields where they feel they have greater scope for their talents. The ones who remain on the whole take more interest in management, as opposed to shop-floor, training. There are training officers who regard management training as the 'glamour' end of their responsibilities. Important as management training is, work is still performed on the shop floor and we ignore the development of shop-floor skills at our peril. Properly conceived training at the workplace can make a substantial contribution, not only to the prosperity of a company, but to the wellbeing of the nation.

In Great Britain, the 1964 Industrial Training Act has altered managers' views about the training function. The levy and grant

3

system has, at least, forced every company to decide 'Are we going to regard the levy only as another overhead cost, or are we going to make an effort to improve our training?' As we shall see later in this book, there is a danger in formulating the question in this form. The process of learning most jobs is expensive, whether the learning process (training) is carried out well or badly. A company could spend unnecessary money attempting to maximize its grant. On the other hand, well-conceived, and not necessarily expensive, shop-floor training may save money and also qualify for grant. It is for senior management to make the primary decision as to how much training should be improved. This book is intended to help them make that decision on a rational basis as far as the training of non-supervisory staff is concerned.

One of the great dangers of the present effervescent situation, in which there is a rush to appoint training staff and produce hastily prepared training schemes in order to maximize grants, is that like all bubbles it is likely to burst. Training staff may feel flattered by the attention now given to their efforts and by the resulting rewards in status and pay; but this period will not last. There will be a demand for positive and practical results. Grants for training will be harder to obtain as the training boards raise their standards. It is vital, therefore, if we are not to enter a period of disillusionment, for managers and training staff to work together closely to ensure that every penny spent on training is wisely used. This cannot be a one-sided responsibility. Training staff must improve their competence and develop their ability to think in management terms. Managers must take the trouble to find out at least the basic principles on which economic and worthwhile training can be founded.

Some of the information required by managers will be found in this book. We have deliberately stressed the need for training to contribute to the profitability of a company in the belief that managers and training staff should think primarily in these terms. Undoubtedly, there are other aspects to training. The improvement of man as a citizen, as a co-operative employee and so on, will in part stem from the efficiency with which he is able to do his job. These are the intangible benefits of training. But there are other benefits, equally important, which can be measured in money terms, which make short-term contributions to improving efficiency and profits. We have concentrated on these in the belief that 'training' can be 'sold' to managers if it can be seen to aid them with their immediate problems. The reader who is looking for a justification of training on anything other than a strictly practical basis will be disappointed. We have used case history material extensively in the belief that one ounce of practical experience is worth several pounds of preaching. However, these case histories are only examples of a principle and what may be a solution in one company is equally likely to be a wrong course of action at a particular moment in time in another. Circumstances vary so much in terms of history, people's personalities, and in what in practice is possible, that a course of action depends on common sense based on understanding of basic ideas and objectives. It is for this reason that, when more than one case has been used to illustrate a point, we have refrained from recommending a 'best buy'.

Skills analysis has tended to become identified with the detailed analysis of manual motions required for mainly repetitive jobs. Today, however, the concept has broadened and we use the phrase in this wider context. To us, skills analysis is concerned with analysing the knowledge and physical skills required by anyone performing a non-supervisory task in industry or commerce. This analysis may be detailed or broad according to circumstances—all that is required is that it should be systematic and detailed enough to form a basis for a sound training programme. Methods of training vary widely. The lecture and a blackboard have their place, so has programmed learning. We only touch on these matters in so far as is necessary to help managers to understand the training process. Detailed evaluation of the various methods of putting over instructions is exhaustively dealt with in other literature. So, too, is the subject of 'skills analysis'. (See W. D. Seymour's books.) We are mainly concerned with how the manager can act upon all this excellent work. In Part I, we show how to assess training need and summarize the things a manager needs to know about training so as to understand the technical aspects of the training officer's task. In Part II, we discuss the role of 'people' in training, particularly the selection, training, and development of the training staff. In Part III, we examine in greater detail the organization of training, while Part IV sums up what a senior manager should do to enable an effective training function to be built up in his company. Like other people, we have our own hobby horses and we have paraded some of them in a final chapter, 'The Future'.

Before getting into detail, it is useful to look at the overall picture. Therefore, the next chapter is a complete case history of one application of skills analysis. It serves as an example of what can be done given the necessary effort by the whole management team.

2. The anatomy of training

We begin the study of the systematic training of non-supervisory personnel with a detailed examination of an application. In this way, we hope your path of exploration will not be completely uncharted, but that every now and then a remembered landmark will come into view. We have chosen, therefore, a case history which indicates many of the pitfalls as well as the triumphs which can occur in developing job skills in an operator workforce. For completeness of understanding, we shall, in this case history, be giving much more background history of the firm than we do in the many other case illustrations that are used throughout this book. The case history, in addition, covers several years of operation ranging from the small beginnings to the present large effort in systematic operator training, in a very cost-conscious organization.

A brief word is in order at this point on the reasons for using case material in the way we do. Firstly, it is our experience that a lot of theory can be talked about management topics. This looks fine on paper, is logical and well argued, and seems to be an elegant presentation of a neat solution to a particular problem area. It is also our experience that enthusiastic and intelligent application of this neat solution can result in only a partial solution of the problem, because of unforeseen difficulties and lack of appreciation of the real-life situation. Numerous examples could be cited from many management topics, but suffice it to mention computer-controlled vehicle scheduling, some incentive payment schemes, some management development approaches, marketing and sales forecasting, product pricing, budgetary control, and so on.

This is not to say that none of these topics has been successfully solved somewhere or other, but rather that there have been dismal failures of application of initial bright theories. If management

6

as a subject is to develop and to be understood, then obviously 'blue skies' thinking is a part of the developing process. We shall try to show by our use of case material that although initially the development of systematic analytical operator training *was* centred on laboratory work, after ten to fifteen years of real-life industrial application, a lot of experience is available about the practical applications of what is basically a very sound theory. The aim of case material is to pass on to the reader the benefit of this hard-won experience.

The second reason for using short sharp case studies is to follow one of the tenets of training which we put forward later on, namely to relate theory to experience, which in this case means industrial experience. Thus, most of the points we make are backed by an apposite snippet of actual practice. The third reason is to demonstrate the generality of this training approach to a wide variety of jobs throughout the whole range of industry, from the hand assembly of microminiature electronic components under microscopes to maintenance on a 10,000-ton press; from shovelling sand to operating a continuous process plant.

The case that follows is concerned with a company we call Universal Products, or U.P. for short, because we shall be revealing the failures as well as the successes in their development of systematic training for non-supervisory personnel.

Background of U.P.

U.P. is an international company with eleven major production units in the United Kingdom and several others located throughout the world. The range of products runs from bespoke one off equipment to highly mechanized mass production of consumer products. The original product on which the company was founded is still a profit producer, but by no means the major product, and accounts for only about 5–10 per cent of sales turnover. U.P. has always been in the forefront of research and has built its growth on developing practical applications of its basic research into mass-produced items. The products have a high reputation for quality and sophisticated design, and in many areas are market leaders. On the human side, the company has an equally high reputation as an enlightened employer with a high degree of job security and competitive rates of pay, especially for hourly paid operatives.

7

Training in U.P.

In the 'fifties, the organization suffered some setbacks in profitability which were due in part to the long lead times being experienced between introducing new products and getting them off the ends of the production lines at an economic forecast volume. The lead times could be anything up to a year, and in several cases competitors jumped in and got similar products on to the market in volume before U.P. This initiative, gained by good design and lost by production holdups, obviously led to loss of sales. Various investigations were made and the conclusion was drawn that the rate of acquisition of skills by assembly operators was one of the main limiting factors. At just about the same time, the research work of W. Douglas Seymour and his team into the acquisition of industrial skills[1] came to the notice of the head of the Central Management Services division through contacts with the Central Personnel Department. The Board was asked to run a pilot study at a small production unit. The particular unit was chosen for the following reasons:

1 It was geographically isolated from any other production unit.
2 It was self-contained with a workforce of about forty girls.
3 The factory manager was very much a paternalistic manager and was very willing to co-operate for the benefit of his girls.
4 The plant was in trouble on the assembly of a new product of a size not previously tackled in the group.
5 There was space available for training, and the plant had a tradition of training new operators using classical methods.
6 Measured day work was in operation with very little disagreement over rates.
7 The effects of failure would not be apparent to other factory managers, but success could be made apparent if so desired.

It had been decided to bring in outside assistance to carry out this pilot study and, when board approval was granted, the consultant started work analysing the skills used by the operators. This took some considerable time, although assistance was given by company personnel. Naturally, impatience was shown by the management who felt that results should be coming out after about a week's work. Results certainly were appearing after a week, but not at this point in time in terms of a dramatic increase in production. The analyst

8

was learning a lot about the problems of analysis on the shop floor of a bunch of girls at home in their own environment. Their reaction varied from the distinctly flirtatious to a mouse-like huddling over the jigs so that not a thing could be observed. Questions by the analyst resulted in either a long circumlocutory discourse or embarrassed giggling, as well as in some very perceptive answers indeed. In all, it took about ten days of continuous shop-floor presence before the analyst was accepted as part of the environment.

The results of the studies done in this unit were developed into a training programme for assembly operators. The form that this programme took varied a great deal from the current successful systematic training being run in the same factory on similar products today. To illustrate this the main items in the two programmes, separated by over ten years of development, are contrasted in Table 2.1.

The most interesting point is the change in emphasis from the research findings of the value of a large number of special exercises, to the practical realization that people like to work on real objects and they like to be able to demonstrate to themselves their ability to make a complete job, even if not at target times. With hindsight, this is fairly obvious, but it should be remembered that at this point in time the principles of systematic training were fairly warm out of the research laboratory. The point should also be made that the 10–12 week training period that was achieved was a considerable improvement on the previous 22–26 weeks to acceptable speed and quality.

Suffice it to say that this pilot study paved the way to further projects for training female assembly operators in other factories in the group, using their own staff with part-time consultancy guidance.

The installation of replicas of the initial training programme went fairly smoothly for a number of years, in most cases being under the control of the work study department. In one major plant, it was run by the plant personnel department but they did not satisfy production's needs. As a result of a board decision, it was reorganized by the work study department with greatly improved results, in this plant at least. The Central Management Services group eventually recruited a team of three or four training specialists who were available to work in any plant to assist in setting up training programmes, or reviewing existing ones, and were also responsible for developing the approach to the benefit of the company.

Table 2.1

	Programme in the 'Fifties	Programme in the Late 'Sixties
Week 1	Introduction to Company. Clock cards Timekeeping Payment Special exercises for $4\frac{1}{2}$ days in $\frac{1}{2}$ hour sessions	Introduction to Company. History Place of unit in total company activities Demonstration of company products Special exercises for 2 days in 15 minute sessions against target times. First element training introduced
Week 2	Special exercises continued against targets Instructress giving demonstrations at target speed Start of job exercises on day 7 Mixture of special exercises and job exercises for rest of week	Element training introduced on total number of 6 elements Special exercises and job exercises as necessary to correct observed trainee difficulties 1 complete job done by end of week Short induction sessions during week
Week 3	Start of element exercises Total number of elements 11 Continuation of element build-up for rest of week	Stamina buildup Completion of induction programme, total of 6 hours Transfer to production conditions set up in training unit
Week 4	Element exercises continued until by middle of week 1 complete stage is attempted Build up of stamina runs for next 4 weeks until target time is reached	Stamina buildup under instructress with feedback of progress and entrance to a sliding guarantee measured day work payment scheme
Week 5 to Week 8	Stamina buildup and return to special exercises where necessary End of period in training unit	Complete handover to production with acceptable speed and quality usually by end of eighth week
Week 8 to Week 12	Handover to production benches and rebuild of speed under production conditions until tempo and quality are acceptable for entry to measured day work payment scheme	

10

Broadening the Application of Training

One of the results of this investment in training expertise was a re-thinking of training policy after about 5-6 years of reasonably successful training experience. Up to that time, U.P. had applied systematic training only in situations which were very similar to the initial exercises, and thus large areas of the group were untouched because the management had got into the habit of thinking that this training approach could only be applied to manual assembly operations and to a very large extent to female operators only. This is perhaps natural in the sense that the plant work study departments and production managements had quite enough to do without having to spend the large amount of time necessary to develop training in fresh areas. The small team of training specialists at the centre had this time and, after some discussions, got the sanction to spend a proportion of their time developing new training programmes.

One of the first of these was concerned with an important subjective or qualitative inspection task where a wrong decision could cause expensive and unnecessary further processing of the product which would then have to be scrapped. Added to this was the fact that the job had a high labour turnover and, although there was an adequate pool of labour, it had no previous traditions in this type of work. It was also an exclusively male job due to the weight of the product being inspected.

Skills analysis principles were still applied with the basic objective of recording how the job was done, but the technique of analysis was very different from observing the manual motions of an assembly operator. The questions that had to be answered were 'how did the inspectors take their decisions?', 'what information did they need?', 'what information were they looking for?', 'how did they perceive this information?—visually, by hearing, by touch, or a combination of all three?' These questions had to be answered by talking to experienced inspectors and by a process of 'bracketing' on a series of products ranging from obviously reject to very high quality to get them to identify the limiting features they perceived in taking their decisions. In other words, the inspectors were helped to set their quality specification in their own operational terms. Having done this and having got production's agreement on the standards, the next thing was to build the training programme.

This was basically a knowledge analysis, but one important point which emerged was that there was a 'best way' of handling the product to be inspected, both for speed, ease of manipulation, and in order to ensure that all surfaces were inspected. The training programme, therefore, was split into two parts, first to make the handling 'automatic' so that no attention need be paid to 'what do I look at next?', and secondly to improve the trainees' perception of the possible faults by inspecting and sorting mixed batches of products ranging from the glaringly obvious to the barely perceptible kind of faults.

The final training programme arrived at employed some novel instructional techniques and was very successful both in terms of reducing training times considerably, reducing labour turnover to well below the factory average, and improving the overall quality of the inspection decisions.

The success of this 'new' application led to whole new areas of training being opened up for consideration and investigation, and this led to further problems. One of the pitfalls in the path of the pioneer is complacency and a tendency to live on past glories. This 'nostalgia syndrome' is one that bedevils training because of its insidious effect. After a couple of years of successful training, there is the temptation to say 'We know it all—look at the visitors who come to learn from us, who come to marvel at our wonderful training units.' What usually happens is that visitors come to learn; they observe politely and then go away and improve greatly on the good basic system they have seen.

This is what had happened in U.P. They had the full backing of the board to hire training staff, training officers, and instructors, and had trained them very well in the techniques of manual assembly operator training using a fixed and proven system. After this initial training, training and development of the training staff had virtually stopped and training tended to become routine and unadventurous. Thus, the impact of new approaches, new instructional techniques, and new areas of profitable activity were blunted because of the inability and, in some instances, latent hostility to change among the training staff accustomed to 5 years of routine administration of laid down techniques.

To cut a long story short, the rebuilding and re-equipping of the training staff, the development of new skills and expertise took about 18 months to 2 years of conferences, training needs analyses, project work, internal and external training courses, job secondment, and the assistance of the central staff for periods of several months in each major plant.

The result of this somewhat painful and certainly time-consuming exercise of increasing the expertise and resources of the training department was the extension of the systematic analysis training approach to an enormous range of tasks, of which the list below is a sample:

Fork lift truck driving.
Continuous process operations.
Order picking in despatch stores.
Product troubleshooting.
Plant troubleshooting.
Vehicle loading.
Subjective inspection tasks.
Quantitative inspection tasks.
Re-skilling for new products.

The next development of interest in U.P. was the export of training knowledge to associated overseas plants. This was done in two ways. First by bringing people on a long secondment, 6 months to 1 year, to the United Kingdom, training them initially, and then giving them a large training project to complete. This method helped the United Kingdom plants because they got work done which would otherwise have been postponed for lack of resources, and the trainees did a real job where the mistakes they made could be discussed and corrected with the central and plant training staff. The second, and less effective way, was to send out a complete training manual with a new product going into an overseas plant. This product would have already been produced in the United Kingdom and the manual was designed for training both instructors and operators. However well the manual was prepared and translated, there were always problems because the managers applying the techniques were doing it from theory and not from guided practice. Another problem was that in some cases a lot of thought had to be given to making special exercises as culture free as possible, especially for developing countries. For example, one special exercise for a subjective inspection task was 'proof reading', a repeating series of specially formulated sentences with deliberate mistakes in them which, after being typed, were photographically reduced in size by a factor of four. This exercise was obviously inappropriate if, first, the trainees were not used to reading English, and second, could not read anyway. One solution was to use shapes, but even here some

13

shapes have, in some cultures, connotations that would never occur to western Europeans.

The important lessons which emerged from the experiences of U.P. can be condensed into a series of key phrases:

Short term use of outside help can be of great assistance in injecting fresh expertise into an organization.

Success must be demonstrated in meaningful, usually financial, terms to naturally sceptical production management.

If training techniques employed have remained unchanged for 2 years, they will almost certainly be capable of improvement, i.e. 'training is dynamic'.

The 'nostalgia syndrome' is an indicator that training is not dynamic.

The training of training staff must be a continuous process; training in a rapidly changing world cannot be routine.

It is highly probable that the skills analysis approach can be profitably applied to a wider range of tasks than you currently think.

Somewhere in the organization there must be people with a full-time responsibility for developing systematic operator training.

Training is a service to production, not a self-contained entity.

The export of technical expertise normally demands practical involvement for successful results.

We have no doubt that you can pull out more points worthy of note from this case study and we sincerely hope you will. We shall, in the succeeding chapters of this book, be expanding these and other points, so with U.P. in mind we hope you will be able to relate the particular with the general as we start to develop the points made in this chapter.

Reference

1 'Experiments on the Acquisition of Industrial Skills': W. D. Seymour.
  Occupational Psychology, April 1954, April 1955, April 1956, January
  1959.

3. The use and evaluation of training

The theme of this book is that training should pay; that it should be seen to be profitable; that it is a management, not a welfare activity. Like other management activities it is necessary to forecast need, plan and implement action, and control results. As T. G. Rose has written[1] 'To measure success, one must first set up some definite objective towards which effort can be directed'. This is the purpose of a training needs analysis—to determine the gap between the present results of the way people learn their jobs, and the desirable results if the learning process were to be improved. It will indicate also the type of training which is most appropriate for a specific operation, and whether systematizing training can make an economic contribution towards the solution of an operating or production problem. How should a line manager initiate the process of assessing training need? Should the first analysis cover all the company or only a part of it? Unfortunately, there can be no cut and dried answer. What is appropriate in one environment may be harmful or wasteful of time and effort in another. Here are a few examples.

A medium-sized company, employing 500 people, had never systematized any of its learning procedures. The Industrial Training Act gave an impetus to rethinking 'training policy'. A comprehensive training needs analysis was carried out to determine whether any benefit would arise from appointing a training officer and preparing a series of systematic training schemes. As a result of this investigation, it was decided that a personnel manager was needed who was able to act also as a training specialist.

In a very large organization, comprising many semi-autonomous

16

units spread throughout the country, the central group training staff had long recognized the need for improving training methods. Before submitting proposals for training a number of people in skills analysis, they carried out a comprehensive assessment of the present training practices in the group to determine the likely payoff which would result if skills analysis based training procedures were widely installed.

In a company employing 4,000 people, training staff found that line management was sceptical of the value of training. Instead of carrying out a detailed analysis which would indicate the total benefit of systematizing training procedures throughout the company, one area of obvious need, where the manager was in general sympathetic to new ideas, was selected. The need for training was established on economic grounds and training improved. The resulting success won the interest of other managers, but before training was improved in any area, an analysis of need was made in that area. At no stage was a comprehensive training needs analysis carried out for the whole company; each area was investigated as the manager became interested. Today, systematic training is widespread throughout the organization.

Another company planned to set up a new factory. Here, the training staff worked closely with other managers to determine the training needs of all employees so that all new entrants would receive training appropriate to their requirements. This was a training needs assessment with a difference because the plant layout and tooling had not been determined finally when the analysis began. The training staff worked in close association with the technical staff and line supervision, training needs being identified as plans developed and were eventually finalized. In this way, 'human error' mistakes were minimized during the vital start up period.

These examples show that there can be no set of rules which must be followed universally when a company decides to investigate its training requirements. In some cases, it may be wise to conduct a thorough investigation; in others, a short analysis of obvious areas may reveal a need sufficient to keep the training staff busy for some time to come. The manager, however, should be guided by two principles:

17

1 The prime need is to improve training—not to carry out an investigation.
2 Investigation is necessary for the following reasons: to set objectives for training and to establish that the cost of systematizing training will be repaid.

Information Required

In order to make more than a cursory assessment of training need, a good deal of detailed information should be obtained. In the following paragraphs, some of the types of information required are outlined and ways of presenting them suggested. A word of warning is needed. In few companies will all the information be readily available and it is unlikely that investigation of every point is required. Much depends on the degree of sophistication of the organization and on the type of work involved. A good deal of common sense is desirable when deciding whether to pursue an investigation of a particular set of statistics. Alternatively, in some cases a detailed investigation of one aspect, even when the facts are not readily available, may reveal the precise information required to make a strong case for training.

Range of Work

A useful starting-point is to determine the kind of tasks people are expected to perform. This has two aspects. First categorize the labour force into broad bands, e.g. different types of maintenance staff, production staff, clerical staff, and so on. Then, examine the broad range of skills required of each group. For example, some groups of production workers may be engaged on repetitive operations, others may be required to produce a wide range of products, operate several types of machine, or use a variety of materials. In some companies, mobility of labour is essential. However, before deciding that everyone has to have multiple skills, check that in practice transfer of workers between jobs is not confined to a few key people who have been in the company for a long period.

The Labour Force

A straightforward breakdown of the labour force by sex, age, and length of service is often useful. It will show whether the labour force is balanced in terms of retirement age, and give a primary indication as to whether it is stable. A possible way of presenting the information is set out in Table 3.1.

Table 3.1

Department and Job	Number M F	Age Under 18	Age 18–30	Age 31–50	Age Over 50	Length of Service Under 1 Year	Length of Service 1–5 Years	Length of Service Over 5 Years
Totals								

Labour turnover statistics, in the majority of cases, should be analysed. Labour turnover is:

$$\frac{\text{Number of leavers in the period (usually 1 year)}}{\text{Average numbers employed}} \times 100 \text{ per cent}$$

These figures need breaking down into major categories of job; for those jobs where turnover is high, a further analysis in the form of a labour stability chart is required. The final form of the chart may be presented as in Table 3.2.

Table 3.2

Job	Number Employed	Length of Service on Leaving Under 6 Months	Length of Service on Leaving 6 Months—1 Year	Length of Service on Leaving 1–3 Years	Length of Service on Leaving Over 3 Years	Turnover Last 12 Months (%)

Often, it is clear that although the majority of employees in a department is stable, the turnover of new starters is very high. Put in a different form, the stability chart will highlight this problem. In this case, it is necessary to go back at least 18 months to the raw personnel records to construct the chart. Suppose we determine the number of people engaged for an operation in January. We can then chart how many *of those engaged* left in each month, i.e. January, February,

19

Table 3.3 NUMBER OF THOSE ENGAGED WHO LEFT IN EACH MONTH

Month	Number Engaged	January	February	March	April	May	June	July	August	September	October	November	December	January	February	March	April
January	20	4	3	5	2	1	0	0	2	0	0	0	1	0	0	0	0	0
February	10	—	2	4	0	2	0	0	1	0	1	0	0	0	0	0	0	0
March	15	—	—	3	5	1	0	4	0	0	0	0	1	0	0	0	0
April	12	—	—	—	2	0	1	0	3	0	1	0	1	0	1	0	0	0
May	16	—	—	—	—	4	4	3	0	2	0	1	0	0	0	0	1	2
June	20	—	—	—	—	—	5	4	2	0	2	0	0	1	0	2	0	2
July	8	—	—	—	—	—	—	1	2	1	3	0	1	0	0	0	0	2
August	11	—	—	—	—	—	—	—	3	2	4	0	0	1	0	0	0	2
September	30	—	—	—	—	—	—	—	—	10	7	3	2	0	1	0	1	4
October	25	—	—	—	—	—	—	—	—	—	8	5	3	4	2	0	1	4
November	10	—	—	—	—	—	—	—	—	—	—	3	1	2	0	1	0	3
December	13	—	—	—	—	—	—	—	—	—	—	—	2	6	4	0	1	16
	190	Totals, Diagonal lines												47	43	29	13	16

March, and so on. We then repeat the process for February starters and so on as shown in Table 3.3.

We can now analyse the diagonal lines. These show that, in the period January–December, of the 190 people engaged:

47 had left in the first month of service
43 had left in the second month of service
29 had left in the third month, and so on.

Put another way, nearly 25 per cent stayed less than 4 weeks, nearly half stayed only 8 weeks, and over 60 per cent had left within 13 weeks of engagement. It is surprising how often an analysis of this kind highlights the real waste of money which is involved in recruiting large numbers of people who only stay a short time. One major factor in this kind of turnover is the difficulty of learning the required skills and the inadequate facilities for training. Managers in this situation often complain that they experience difficulties in recruitment.

They are wrong: the real problem is retaining people they have recruited. Improved selection and training arrangements can contribute greatly to the solution of this difficulty. The labour stability chart in Table 3.3 may show also that recruits leave at a certain point in their training. In one firm, for example, few people left during the formal training period, but a large percentage left on transfer to the shop floor and piecework conditions. This is another certain

20

indication that the training given was unsatisfactory and inadequate to meet production needs.

Present Performance of Operators

Training is complete only when the learner can produce, in terms of output and quality, at a standard comparable with that of an experienced worker. The training needs analysis must determine, therefore, what this standard is. Sometimes, this is a simple matter of charting the average of the last 4 weeks' earnings or the production figures for each operator, or that of a sample of experienced operators. In other cases, it may be necessary to assess subjectively the knowledge and skill which an experienced worker possesses, though in most cases it is possible to determine what distinguishes the experienced from the inexperienced in terms of production figures.

Individual analysis of operator production records can reveal interesting data. It may, for example, highlight a retraining problem or indicate that there are two stages in the current learning process, as where a small group is capable of high production, a large group produces some 10–20 per cent less, and the remainder are at varying stages of proficiency. It is then necessary to determine what steps could be taken to help the middle group to achieve the higher standards of the best operators.

Length of Present Training

The length of the present training is the time taken to achieve an experienced worker's standard, NOT the time to be able to perform the job at all, or just earn piecework minimum with no makeup. Where individual production records are kept, this 'learning graph' can be charted in the way shown in Table 3.4.

Table 3.4

Name of New Starter	Production on Each Week After Engagement (Units of Production)																	
	1	2	3	4	5	6	7	8	9	10	11	12	13	14	15	16	17	18
A	15	25	36	42	40	42	50											
B	20	30	35	43	40	43	50											
C	10	15	29	37	42	45	55											
D	15	20	30	40	36	40	45				etc.							
E	17	23	30	38	40	38	44											
F	13	25	32	40	36	44	50											
Total	90	138	192	240	234	252	294											
Average (Total)/6	15	23	32	40	39	42	49	55	60	63	70	72	80	78	84	86	90	90

Fig. 3.1 A typical learning graph

Assuming an experienced worker's standard is 90 units per week, these figures can then be graphed as in Fig. 3.1. This is a typical learning graph for many industrial operations. The interested reader can find other examples in W. D. Seymour's book *Industrial Training for Manual Operations*.[2] The interesting feature of most learning graphs is the relatively short period required to achieve a satisfactory level of quality performance, and the long period of further experience necessary to attain the output standards of the average experienced worker.

Current Cost of Training

Calculation of the current cost of training must take into account the loss of production which is suffered because learners have not yet achieved experienced workers' standard. They may be covering their basic wage in terms of output, but the company is suffering in terms of lost productive capacity.

Some other factors to take into account are the cost of excess scrap or rectification work required because of poor trainee performance, the cost of labour turnover, as well as the direct costs incurred in teaching learners.

The extent to which any of these, or other indicators, require analysis depends on the situation. Take, for example, the labour stability chart in Table 3.3. If we assume that learners produce little saleable work in the first 2 months, ninety people were paid wages, and incurred overheads, for no return during the year. Assuming an average length of stay of 4 weeks for these ninety people, and a direct wage cost £12 0s. 0d. per week for each person, the cost involved is 90 × 4 × £12 0s. 0d. = £4,320 0s. 0d. This is by no means an untypical figure in a unit employing several hundred people where trainee labour turnover is high, and takes no account of the cost of lost production, the tying up of space or machinery, and other 'hidden' factors.

Present Training Arrangements

An analysis of training need must take into account the way in which people currently learn their jobs. If instructors are used, have they been taught how to teach, what kind of analysis of skill and knowledge required has been undertaken, and do the instructors work to a timetable? It is also important to find out whether there are any systematic checks on trainee progress both for management control purposes and to enable the learner to assess the progress he is making towards the goal of an experienced worker's standard.

General Production Background

As we shall see later, a problem that appears to be one of a lack of systematic training arrangements may be due to other factors which lie deeper in the organization. Therefore, it is necessary to examine the general production background against which people have to learn their jobs. Some of the questions which need to be asked are:

Does supervision recognize the need to improve the current learning arrangements?
How is the flow of work organized?
How is work inspected and quality insured?
How are instructions given to operators?
How is machinery serviced, and are there any preventive maintenance procedures?
What are the raw materials used in the work? Do they vary in quality?
What are the pay arrangements?

These, and other related questions, will ensure that any proposals for improving training are made within the general production framework. Training is not an end in itself—its improvement is only relevant in so far as it makes a contribution to solving a production problem. Unfortunately, there are cases where first-class training has been of little value because other factors have largely nullified the expected benefits.

Recruitment and Selection Arrangements

There is little point in improving training if the quality of the trainees is such that they do not possess the basic aptitudes to benefit from it. It is worthwhile checking, therefore, that some screening process is used to ensure the correct quality of intake. Production pressures often lead managers to accept any recruit, however unlikely his subsequent successful performance may be. This is really the triumph of hope over experience, which shows that most people taken on in this way fail to make the grade. Not only is this a waste of money, but often departmental morale suffers. A surer solution is to select and to train well, for then the need to recruit large numbers lessens and labour turnover decreases.

Accident Rates

In some industries, accident rates are excessive. The training needs analysis should consider whether accidents can be reduced by better training. One indicator is to determine the relationship between accident rates and length of service on the job. If most accidents occur to people who have been on the job a short time, then poor training is probably a large contributory factor.

Machine Utilization

One possible cause of low machine utilization is excessive downtime resulting from the lack of skill or experience of setters or operators. It is useful to determine the exact extent of unproductive machine time expressed as a percentage of theoretical running time. This can be done in the following way.

Assume the machine can run 80 hours each week. If it never stopped it would produce, say, 1,200 units. However, certain stoppages are planned, e.g. changeover time and preventive maintenance time. Allowances for these factors reduces theoretical production to, say, 1,000 units. Now determine how many units were produced. An analysis of the causes of the lost production may suggest a training problem.

Quality Information

Some of the questions which relate to quality are:

Is there a quality specification for the stage in the process of manufacture under examination? In other words, how do new operators discover what quality standard is expected of them?
What are the quality standards of experienced operators and are they satisfactory?
Do quality standards vary with customer or seasonal requirements? In this connection, it is necessary to find out whether they vary in practice, rather than in theory.
Are new operators training to meet the quality standards required in practice, or are they set too high a standard which does not mirror 'what the man on the shop floor can get away with'?

This last question can be very important, because if learners are trained to a higher standard of quality attainment than that expected of the group in which they will work, the subsequent drop in quality suffered while they adjust to 'real-life' standards can be very expensive.

Present Learning Difficulties

All aspects of a job are not equally difficult to master. During the analysis of training need, it is necessary to assess the length of time it will take to analyse the job and prepare a training course, and to determine the new length of training time required. To make the initial assessment, observations should be made of trainees or of substandard workers. Look particularly for:

Hurried or erratic movements.
Excessive rechecking of movements made or of decisions taken.
Excessive 'thinking' time.

Then, relate these to the way experienced operators perform. Translating these factors into 'analysis' and 'training' time is more difficult. The experienced training specialist tends to draw on his past experience of similar situations. The following very rough guide may be helpful. Where the length of training time up to experienced worker's standard is under 6 months, the revised training time, using skills analysis, will be about half. The amount of analysis time required will be roughly half the revised training time.

This is a long list of 'information required'. Not all of it is relevant to every situation, but the training needs analysis should continue to the point where the analyst has sufficient information to make a sound case for improving the current training, and has sufficient detailed knowledge to argue it forcefully.

The Training Problem Which Wasn't

Described below are three cautionary tales.

In a large machine-shop, very few orders seemed to be made on time. Supervision and management were convinced of one primary cause—lack of training. Managements stated that supervisors, setters, and operators all needed training; supervisors stated that the setters and operators needed training. Investigation showed that these statements were indeed true, but the primary cause of the recurring production crises was to be found in the almost total lack of any proper production planning arrangements. In this situation, money spent solely on improving setter and operator training would have been in vain.

In a factory making television screens, an operator at the end of a conveyor belt was required to sort the product in accordance with the coloured tags on the screens. Not an exacting task, but the operator seemed unable to grasp what was required of him. In desperation, the training department was called in to help to train the man. No training was necessary—all that was required was to replace the existing operator with one who was not colour blind!

In an engineering works, the general level of output was poor. Management commissioned a training needs analysis, which did reveal that the training arrangements could be improved. However, the first need was to improve morale which was poor because of frequent changes of orders, badly maintained and inadequate machinery, and a lack of leadership from above. In this situation, training needed to start at the top—not at the bottom of the hierarchy.

Using the Training Needs Assessment

Assuming the assessment of training needs reveals a weakness in the current training arrangements, an estimate of the cost/effectiveness of the anticipated improvements should be undertaken. In these days of grant and levy from Training Boards, the following formula is useful:

The present cost of training + the levy
should be less than
The savings from improving training + the grant.

Estimating the savings from improved training involves calculating the excess costs incurred by having to train people and deciding how much they are likely to be reduced. This obviously cannot be an exact calculation, but some reasonable estimates are possible. Take, for example, the three major loss factors:

Excessive labour turnover.
Lost production.
Excess scrap or rectification.

On page 22, we have already carried out a calculation of the cost of high labour instability. Experience of similar situations would show

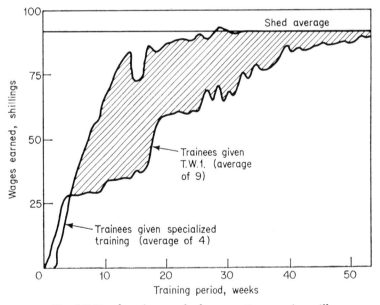

Fig. 3.2 Two learning graphs from a cotton weaving mill

27

that this excess cost figure of £4,320 0s. 0d. could be reduced by at least two thirds. In the example quoted, further calculations would be made to show the excess cost of people leaving within 6 months of engagement, though in this case direct wages would have to be offset by the value of production. Even so, reducing the labour turnover by half would produce substantial savings. The calculation of lost production can be tackled in a number of ways.

In the chart in Fig. 3.2, two learning graphs from a cotton weaving mill are reproduced.[3] The cross hatched portion of the chart indicates the increased production achieved by each trainee during his first year in the company. It is possible to convert this figure into money. Although this is an actual achieved example, a prediction could have been made that the old training time would be reduced to 26 weeks and a 'theoretical' new learning graph drawn from which calculations could be made.

Another method, useful in machine work, is to calculate the value of increased production resulting from each 1 per cent in reduction of down time. Here, again, experience shows that improved training of setters and operators will result in at least 5 per cent reduction in downtime where the present machine utilization, after allowing for changeovers and planned maintenance, is between 70 and 85 per cent.

Excess costs due to scrap and rectification vary enormously with the type of product and stage of the process. Often, they are significant. Excess costs resulting from poor trainee work should be reduced by effective training by as much as 50 per cent.

Against these savings must be set the capital cost of analysing the job in order to prepare the training course. This is a once only operation, while the savings accrue each year. Another capital cost may be the provision of a training centre, if the training is not to be carried out on the shop floor. Sometimes, a calculation is made of the instructor's wages, but this in many cases may be disregarded because, even with traditional exposure methods, someone has to spend time showing starters what to do, and pointing out their mistakes.

Relationship with Manpower Planning

The assessment of training needs is greatly affected by the future manpower needs of the company. One of the most significant factors is technological change. The progress towards more mechanization and automation, however gradual, implies that in the future men will be paid more for their mental skills than for physical dexterity. In the short run, training or retraining may be required to give new knowledge to existing workers, but in the longer term many companies need to consider whether their present apprenticeship arrangements will meet the needs of the future. How many craftsmen and technicians will be needed? What syllabus of training should they be given? Can better training reduce present learning times so that more can be taught in the same period of apprenticeship?

The training needs for new factories also require careful consideration. All employees will need some form of induction training; many will require job training. A detailed syllabus of the skills required should be compiled and matched against skills available in the area where the factory is to be opened. No easy assumptions should be made because there are always surprises.

A company planned to open a new factory in a development area. They knew that a pool of engineering craftsmen existed and expected that little job training would be required, as opposed to a short period of familiarization. Fortunately, job analysts and selection staff worked closely together, for the latter were able to explore in detail how many of the specific skills required were really possessed by applicants. One of these skills was the ability to read a micrometer speedily and accurately. Few of the applicants possessed this skill to the required standard because the type of work in the area made the use of an inch rule more appropriate than a micrometer.

The moral is to leave nothing to chance. The smooth opening and build up of production in a new factory depends to a large extent on how rapidly everyone acquires the specific skills needed. It is often worthwhile training these systematically rather than assuming an underlying previous experience which may be missing.

Anticipated changes in the product may also present training challenges. New skills may be required; the training analyst should determine the exact differences in skill and knowledge required between the old and the new product. If these are significant, then people will have to learn new things and if large numbers are involved, then it may be worthwhile training systematically. As consultants, we are often astonished at the length of time managers will allow before a new production line can be said to be working satisfactorily. In many cases, the time could have been much reduced if some elementary training principles had been applied.

Finally, the training needs analysis and manpower forecast need to take account of external factors. Some of these are:

Will the availability of labour be affected by new factories opening in the area?

What difference is the raising of the school leaving age likely to make? This may be particularly important where large numbers of females are employed. There is an increasingly narrowing gap between school leaving and marriage. Greatly accelerated training may be required to maintain the period of a female operator's working life as an experienced worker.

What is the likely long-term effect of the Industrial Training Act and the national manpower forecasts? Is it likely to be more difficult to recruit certain types of labour?

Resources Needed

Finally, where a case has been made for improving training, an estimate must be made of the resources required to implement the changes required. How many analysts and instructors will be needed? Should they be full time or part time? The number of analysts required depends on the speed with which management wishes to introduce systematic training, while the number of instructors depends on the number of anticipated trainees. For most jobs, a ratio of one instructor to eight trainees is required. Increasing the ratio means that each learner cannot receive the individual tuition he needs, thus lengthening the training period and increasing training costs.

An estimate should also be made of the equipment needed for training and whether a training centre should be provided. We return to this subject in more detail in chapter 6.

It should now be clear that, before training can be improved, certain steps should be taken to ensure that any training is relevant to management's needs and that the cost of improvement does not out-weigh the likely savings. The preparation of a training needs assessment is a management activity normally carried out by training staff. In the next chapter, we consider in more detail the technical aspects of training and answer the question 'Why is it that skills analysis pays?'

References

1 *The Mensuration of Management:* T. G. Rose. Monograph No. 3.
2 *Industrial Training for Manual Operations:* W. D. Seymour. Pitman, 1954.
3 By permission of the Cotton Board Productivity Centre.

4. The need to analyse skill

So far we have discussed training in isolation, in general terms and not related to the individual. What we have to consider is the meaning of training to the individual from the viewpoint of the way in which he learns.

Theories about the way in which people learn are legion, and Hilgard's book[1] gives a very full account of both current and past theories of learning. However, in industrial training and particularly operator training, there is not enough time nor expertise to discuss the finer points of differing theories of learning. What industrial training is looking for is hard cash results and the best method of applying what is known about learning *in practice*. Accordingly, we are going to talk theory in terms of observable results and to do this we are going to look at an observable phenomenon we call insight.

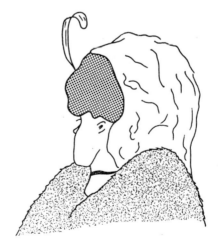

Fig. 4.1 The old woman/young woman illusion

In looking at the drawing in Fig. 4.1, you will see, in all probability, a face. This may be of an old woman, her chin sunk into her chest, a big nose, and wearing a headscarf tucked into the collar of a fur coat. On the other hand, other readers may see a young lady wearing a necklace, a flowing turban sort of hat, and looking over her right shoulder. In most cases, you will see immediately one or other of these portraits. Now try to see the other face.

You have no doubt found it difficult to see the second face, but the drawings in the Appendix to this chapter may help you. (See page 45.) Suddenly, the second face appears and you wonder why you could not see it immediately. What has happened is that you have gained insight into the task of seeing two faces from the same arrangement of black lines on white paper. In other words, you have seen with your eyes this arrangement of black lines, but initially you perceived only one picture with your brain. After gaining insight into the task, you perceived or organized with your brain the single pattern of lines into two possible meaningful pictures. Beauty is in the eye of the beholder or more correctly in the perception of the beholder.

The experiment you have just conducted is directly analogous to operator training and helps to explain operator training at a basic and individual level. Operator training is giving insight to productive personnel into the tasks assigned to them in order that they can undertake those tasks with speed, quality, accuracy, and ease. How then do we provide this insight and supply it effectively and economically?

There are two major methods of training operators; by exposure to the task, commonly called 'sit by Nellie' or 'stand by Jack', or by analytical techniques of which T.W.I. job breakdowns and skills analysis are the two major examples. We are for the moment not considering programmed instruction, although it is based on analytical techniques and is in many situations a good method of imparting knowledge or brain skills to a trainee. It should be added at this point that we are positive that programmed instruction has and will have a large part to play in certain areas of systematic operator training.

Exposure methods of operator training depend upon the trainee being able to observe and to perceive the key elements of a task with the minimum of outside help or guidance. This makes it a rather chancy affair, as people in general are very poor observers. They see things but do not necessarily perceive them and certainly do not always remember them. If you wish to demonstrate this, see Fig. 4.2

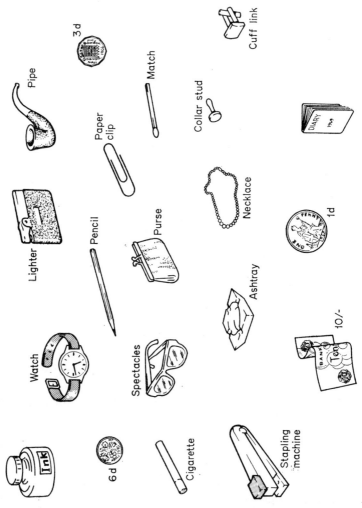

Fig. 4.2 Kim's game: traditional layout

Instructions: Look at for one minute then list all objects from memory

34

Fig. 4.3 Kim's game: systematic training equivalent

Note: The objects are placed in related groups for ease of learning

35

for the old scout exercise called Kim's game and Fig. 4.3 for its systematic training equivalent.

In a precision engineering company making products for the automotive industry, fuel injection nozzles were being hand lapped on their inside bore to a very high degree of finish and narrow dimensional tolerances using a rotary lap. Training using upgraded 'sit by Nellie' methods with an instructor took about a year to achieve experienced worker's standard. After examination of the task, the skills analyst discovered that the key skill was to perceive the torque of the rotary lap cutting metal through the pressure on and deflection of the thumb-tip holding the work. The result of transmitting this insight immediately to new trainees was to reduce training time to a maximum of 1 month.

The key point in the above case is the phrase, 'after examination of the task by the skills analyst' and its result. That is to say, the task to be accomplished is examined by a trained observer, the skills analyst, not by an untrained observer, the trainee. This, then, is the first factor in the skills analysis approach:

Work skills are analysed by a trained observer.

Josef Pieper, in his *Introduction to Thomas Aquinas*,[2] makes a point about teachers which could equally well have been written about the good skills analyst: 'He sees the reality just as the beginner can see it, with all the innocence of the first encounter, and yet at the same time with the matured powers of comprehension and penetration that the cultivated mind possesses.' The time and cost involved in analysing work prior to training 'with the matured powers of comprehension' are amply repaid by significant training benefits.

The second major factor in the skills analysis approach is the way in which the information collected by the trained observers is transmitted to the trainees. In the exposure method, trainees are normally given the task in one big chunk, i.e. they are learning by the 'whole' method of learning. Skills analysis, on the other hand, feeds the amount to be learned by the trainee in small logical stages and the trainee learns the job in steps.

The 'part' method of learning, as this is called, ensures that the trainee is not swamped with new information to be learned, but is presented with the fresh knowledge in easily absorbed elements.

36

The difference between 'whole' and 'part' methods of learning can be illustrated by taking the analogy of learning a ten verse poem. The 'whole' method of learning would involve learning all ten verses at once, probably by continuously reading through the whole poem. By the 'part' method, the procedure would be to learn the first one or two verses off by heart and then, and only then, to proceed to the next one or two verses and so on, until the whole poem has been learned.

In summary, therefore, a second major factor in the skills analysis approach is that: After the complete job to be trained has been analysed, it is then broken up into sections which are trained to experienced worker's standard individually before being combined into the whole job. The important decision where training is concerned is to establish the size of each part to be learned. Basic analysis is, in this case, the decisive factor.

This is so particularly for skills analysis of manual motions, where it is normally fairly easy to examine the analysis and to identify each portion or element of the job which involves a new skill. The new skill can be an uncommon manual motion with one or both hands, an unusual combination of controlling senses, a combination of foot and hand motions, or some necessary perceptual skill.

In some cases, these training elements will match exactly work study elements, but it should be remembered always that we are looking for points of difficulty from a training, not a method study, viewpoint. The difference is often significant. In knowledge or brain skill analysis, the less quantitative nature of the data makes it less easy to identify points of difficulty from the basic analysis and requires more interpretative skill on the part of the analyst.

The golden rule here is to tend towards more training elements than are strictly necessary, rather than too few, and then, if necessary, modify the initial assessment of training elements in the light of actual training experience. We shall deal in greater detail with this point in the next chapter. We can summarize at the moment with: Points of difficulty are generally identified by examination of the basic analysis. The initial identification may be modified by actual training experience.

In answer to the question 'What is skills analysis?', it is sufficient at this stage to say: Skills analysis is the observation of work skills by a trained observer. These skills are then taught, using carefully devised and proved training methods, which take into account the manner in which individuals acquire new skills. We shall develop this brief statement in the course of the following chapters, so that a total approach to non-supervisory industrial training is demonstrated.

At this point, however, it would be useful to set out brief case studies to illustrate the range of industrial tasks where skills analysis has been applied successfully. The cases have been classified in two ways, by types of industrial task and by types of industry using the categories employed by Joan Woodward.[3] These categories can overlap, but each is useful and has its place.

Manual Task

A small company assembling lighting fittings had problems of high labour turnover and low production rate. Working conditions were good and rates were set by using a well tried predetermined time system applied by very experienced industrial engineers. Assembly was done manually in jigs and fixtures by women using simple air tools and hand tools. A few operators could make the rate easily and payment was above average for the area, using a high day-rate system. The problem of high labour turnover was not caused by labour shortage as a sister plant, 1½ miles away, had no difficulty in recruiting and retaining labour. Current training times were difficult to determine as few people stayed long enough to reach acceptable production speeds and quantity. The tasks were analysed and the common skills identified because a wide variety of types of fittings were being made. A training section was set up and a complete assembly team trained from scratch in two weeks' training time. At this point, trainees were producing at acceptable production speeds and quality. All of them stayed more than six months and seven out of eight stayed more than twelve months.

Machine Controlled Task

In the coil winding department of an electrical engineering company, production of the machines was limited because operators could not complete the necessary preparation work during the automatically controlled portion of the machine cycle. In other words, their process time tasks were taking too long and, therefore, machine idle time was excessive. Analysis of the whole job showed that operators were taking too long deciding when to stop the automatic winding cycle, which had to be done by the operator, because they were unsure of how to tell when the machine was approaching the end of a specified number of winds. This meant they kept stopping the machine, checking the windings counter, starting it again, stopping it and so on, until the correct number of winds were laid. Some experienced operators could stop a machine from full speed and, within the specified limits, have the correct number of winds.

The analysis of the experienced operators showed that the key skill they possessed was the ability to hear and register the 'tens' counter clicking over and count these to the correct number of winds. They also knew that braking the machine by hand with a certain pressure meant that they had to allow a certain number of winds for this braking period. The experienced workers could also make fairly accurate estimates of time passing, i.e. they could say to within one or two seconds when a minute had passed.

Having identified these skills, the other less efficient operators were retrained as well as new trainees, and the overall effect was to increase the output of the coil winding department with the same labour force. This was a true increase in productivity as for the same input there was a greater output.

Maintenance and Setting Task

In an integrated steel rolling mill, the company estimated that the cost of downtime was £100 per minute in lost saleable product. Some downtime was, of course, unavoidable, but this was aggravated by what the engineering management considered excessive fault-finding and rectification time by the maintenance engineering staff. The solution to this problem lay in producing a faults analysis and faults diagnosis using skills analysis, and then using this categorized information to train the maintenance fitters in logical fault-finding as opposed to their previous methods of hit and miss. These hit and miss methods in some cases consisted of removing and replacing a relay or a valve at random and then seeing if the equipment worked. The time taken to do this sort of analysis is considerable, but is economic when it is remembered that one hour per week saved in downtime is worth £300,000 ($720,000) per year to the company.

Inspection Task

In an inspection department, where the task was to inspect visually television screens which had been polished prior to being joined to the cone, training was taking 12 to 14 weeks with a high labour turn-over during training. Although it was a small department in numbers, there was a continuing training task which affected morale within the department and therefore its production performance. The analysis of the task showed that two distinct types of skills were required. First, large and heavy TV screens had to be handled manually to ensure inspection of all surfaces. Secondly, pattern recognition skills were required to perceive faults such as air bubbles, scratches, sleeks, bruises, and dust embedded in the glass. These faults would often be very small in size and difficult to see.

By training the trainees first to handle the glass in a fixed sequence until it was 'automatic', and then, and only then, bringing in fault and pattern recognition, it was possible to cut to a maximum of 4 weeks the training times required to attain experienced worker's standard. This was due to the fact that the trainees could concentrate now all their attention on perceiving faults from graded exercises in the second part of their training without having to think, 'Which way do I turn the glass now?'

Clerical Task

A distribution company had a tape-controlled typewriter system for preparing invoices and stock record cards. The efficiency of this system depended on the accuracy of address card selection and the tape-punching ability of the operators. The overall speed of produc-tion was important because all invoices and stock records had to be prepared in batches by certain times of the day.

The requirements of the training programme had to be achieved as quickly as possible because the female labour used was switched around from job to job. There was a fairly high labour turnover resulting from the geographical isolation of some of the depots. Each depot had one or more automatic typewriters, and it was considered uneconomical to spend much time and money on training this grade of labour.

The analysis of the few experienced operators available showed that they all had large amounts of spare capacity, i.e. when the occasion demanded they could increase output. The training programme devised depended for its success on the selection of trainees according to criteria disclosed by the analysis. These criteria included manual dexterity, pattern recognition for reading handwritten order forms, and an even, unambitious temperament for a highly repetitive and sometimes frustrating task. The programming of practice times on the machines, when it was known the machines would not be in use, also assisted in reducing the effects on regular production and the cost of training, as it avoided buying or setting aside machines for purely training purposes.

Technical Supervisor's Task

An ethical pharmaceutical firm has in many of its more technical departments 'working chargehands'. It also practises job rotation among its junior supervisory staff, so there is a constant training requirement both in the supervisory aspects and in the technical side of the jobs. In one section of this firm, the chargehand was responsible for batching, mixing, and quality controlling the production of tablets, which were then sent to a packing section. The analysis of his task showed that he had to have a considerable knowledge of the factors involved in mixing and batching, ostensibly laboratory and specification controlled, which affected the tableting machines. Examples of this were the effect of humidity, moisture content, and grain size on the strength and weight of the tablets and whether they would form at all on the die pressing tableting machines.

As a result of the analysis, the company had the opportunity to improve supervisory performance to lessen machine downtime, and reduce loss of product. The main factor, however, was the analysts' recognition that the major tasks of the supervisor were of a technical nature, not man-management as he was only responsible for two labourers. Previously, much of the supervisor's training had been concerned with 'human relations' aspects.

Small Batch Industry

In a hosiery company making underwear, nightwear, and similar products in batches of a dozen, a batch could be any one of a large variety based on size, materials, or design. The firm already had a training section for sewing machinists using an advanced form of T.W.I. job instruction with a type of special exercise. In principle, this training was well thought out, although the results achieved were not up to the expectations of production management. The tasks of flat machinists and overlockers were analysed in detail, and it was discovered that some necessary skills were not being taught by the

41

current training method. Examples of these skills were cloth or garment handling to the machine, the skills of folding and lining up four or five layers of cloth, machine speed control, and machining in difficult confined areas, usually occurring when the garment was almost complete.

It was established also that the special exercises used were not teaching the skills in use on the shop floor. That is to say, the trainees were acquiring the skills of doing the special exercises very well but these skills were of little use on the shop floor. Having identified the required skills, the training programme was developed using more appropriate special exercises. The performance of trainees on reaching the production floor was most acceptable to the production management.

Medium Batch Industry

A construction company engaged in driving foundation piles in numbers varying from 20–1,000 on any one site used skills analysis to prepare a training programme for its teams of four who operated each of its pile driving rigs. The task took 8 days to analyse using two analysts, because of the problems of relating simultaneous activities by two or more members of the team.

From the analysis, the skills of the various team members were isolated: for example, the way in which the winchman operated his clutches and brakes during the actual hammering of the piles, the skills of the topmen in locating the anvil or changing driving tubes, and, very importantly, the skills of co-operation and communication required by each team member in order to achieve speed of production with safety. The programme produced from the analysis enabled a team to be trained in weeks instead of the previous training time of months.

Mass Production Industry

In a company making semiconductors on a mass-production basis, for the final assembly of the component parts prior to 'canning' there was the problem of a long slow climb to required production speeds with 'learning plateaux' occurring. This led to a proportion of female trainees leaving after 3 or 4 months under training, which meant that training was very expensive for the company. The job was done under binocular microscopes because of the minute size of the components.

It tended to be a very frustrating task because of the precision nature of the work, for example, having to position three wires on to a silicon chip the size of a full stop.

The analysis was carried out with some difficulty as it was not easy to observe exactly what the girls' hands were doing under a binocular microscope. This problem was solved eventually by fixing an additional eyepiece to the microscope and filming the operators, as well as by direct observation by the analyst. Two major results ensued from the investigation. First, it was clear that careful selection of trainees was vital and the analysis helped to specify the criteria for better selection. Secondly, that it was essential to get the girls as quickly as possible to work under microscopes.

A subsidiary result was that the training officer was able to decide after 2 weeks' training, on the basis of the data provided by the analysis, whether a girl was really suited to this kind of work. The development of special exercises and selection tests for manual dexterity, degree of hand tremor, and spatial perception helped not only to reduce training time, but also to reduce considerably the loss of trainees towards the end of an expensive training period.

Process Industry

A firm engaged in the extrusion of thin-walled plastic tube suffered a loss in productivity due to long changeover times between different diameters or colours of tubing, and incurred high scrap losses. The process consisted of feeding a thick liquid plastic through an extrusion head, on to a mandrel, both of which were submerged in an opaque setting solution. The tube thus formed was washed, dried, and cured, and eventually put on to reels ready for despatch. The process from extrusion to reeling was continuous, and in the factory there were several sets of equipment so that different types of tube could be produced simultaneously. The machines were operated by teams of three men, each team being responsible for two sets of equipment.

The analysis showed that the key skills were the cleaning and initial setting of the extrusion dieheads. Another key skill was starting a new tube which had to be guided over the mandrel and then run through various rollers, washing baths, and drying frames, until the reeling machine was reached. The final setting of the diehead was done completely blind, after the tube had been successfully started, by adjusting three screws on the face of the diehead which was wholly immersed in the black setting solution. It was in the setting of the

43

diehead and in starting the tube that the greatest time and product losses were being experienced.

The training programme which was developed from the analysis materially assisted in reducing these time and product losses. Special exercises and simple simulators were used to train the identified skills before operators were transferred to the actual production equipment.

These ten case outlines are designed to give some idea of the scope of skills analysis. Some of the studies will be presented in greater detail to illustrate particular points of special exercises, training techniques, or problems of analysis that we make in the two chapters following.

References

1 *Theories of Learning:* E. R. Hilgard, Second edition, Methuen, 1958.
2 *Introduction to Thomas Aquinas:* Josef Pieper, Faber & Faber, 1962.
3 *Industrial Organization: Theory and Practice:* J. Woodward, Oxford University Press, 1965.

Appendix

An explanation of the old woman/young woman illusion in Fig. 4.1

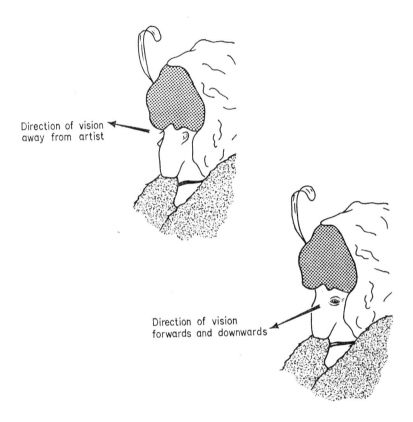

Direction of vision
away from artist

Direction of vision
forwards and downwards

5. Design of training

In the last chapter, we looked at the background and scope of skills analysis, giving some examples of typical installations. In the next two chapters, which complete Part I of the book, we shall examine in more detail what skills analysis involves from the time of deciding to analyse a task for training purposes to the stage of having a training programme prepared and ready to run. This present chapter is concerned, in particular, with two key steps in the design of systematic non-supervisory training.

Analysis and Synthesis

At first sight, the two processes of analysis, that is, breaking down into parts, and synthesis, or putting together, are direct opposites and as such cancel each other out. But if we think of synthesis as the molecular chemists look at it, synthesis means rebuilding elements or constituents in a new or an alternative way to that of the original construction. Thus, nowadays, it is possible to design and to build penicillins to meet a wide range of medical needs by synthesis of basic building blocks, forming different chemical links for different purposes. The synthesis of analysed skills in systematic industrial training is carried out in a similar way. Thus, synthetics in our terms may properly be defined as rebuilding a whole from analysed elements in a way dictated not by the obvious methods but by the needs of training. In other words, the end result is the same, the task is completed, but the method of achieving it is adapted to training requirements.

Analysis

As described in the previous chapter, the first step in systematic industrial training is the analysis and recording of the skills to be taught. There are three main headings under which skills can be categorized, and each of these has its own problems and its own techniques available to solve them. Perhaps, historically, the area of skill about which most is known and where the greatest experience is available is that of physical skills. It is appropriate, therefore, to start with physical skills although, as we shall see, in this chapter and the final chapter, the other two areas of job knowledge and 'brain' skills are steadily gaining in importance as industrial manufacturing processes change their nature.

Physical skills are concerned with complex co-ordination of muscular movements by the use of the receptor senses such as vision, hearing, touch, kinaesthesia, either singly or in combination. As an everyday example of a physical skill we can take walking.

In walking, the muscular movements are rather complex because of the large number of groups of muscles that have to operate in a co-ordinated manner, such as foot muscles, leg and thigh muscles, back muscles, neck and shoulder muscles, and arm muscles. Learning to co-ordinate all this muscular activity is quite difficult, as anyone watching a baby learning to walk will agree. The necessary control information comes in continuously from several senses: vision in locating obstacles and helping to give a frame of reference for balance; touch for the information about the kind of surface you are walking on, e.g. carpets or ice; kinaesthesia, for information about where the limbs are in space; hearing as an additional cue for the kind of surface, especially when changes occur, e.g. grass to pavements. The list obviously can be extended if you consider special types of walking such as with an artificial leg, or in the case of a blind person, or up steep hills, or on treacherous surfaces. From the training point of view, walking for the vast majority of the human race is a complex but overlearned skill. That is to say, it has been relegated to the level that does not require conscious thought except in some extreme cases such as on a tightrope or an ice-covered slope.

This outline demonstrates some of the things that have to be analysed if physical skills are to be understood for training purposes. In general, the analysis should contain:

1 A description of the muscular movements involved, in what combination and in what sequence.
2 A breakdown of the primary control senses for the identified muscular movements.

47

One of the advantages of muscular movements is that they can be observed, which makes the first stage of the analysis comparatively easy. There are, of course, certain pitfalls and booby traps set for the unwary who observe physical skills and try to record them. The most troublesome have been:

1 Speed of movements, 'the quickness of the hand deceives the eye'.
2 Difficulty of observation due to working position, size of product, number of repetitions of a given cycle, safety problems, working space available, attitudes of experienced operators, and such environmental problems as noise, heat, dust, and lighting.
3 Difficulties in recording quickly and accurately what is observed.
4 Time taken by the need to see an operation carried out several dozen times before a clear breakdown is obtained.
5 Observer fatigue and loss of concentration while observing work.
6 Danger of missing bits of the analysis or adding bits twice if the analysis is done in sections, because of any of the reasons given above. This is apparent at the beginning and end of job cycles.
7 Variations in methods used by operators.

The first problem, speed of movement, can be tackled in several ways. Obviously, the operator being observed can be asked to slow down, but this has its dangers. High speed skills differ greatly from low speed skills. A second approach, if economically justified, is to film it at high speed and then slow the action down by use of the projector speeds. A variation of this is to use closed circuit television with a video recorder, which has the advantage of immediacy of playback, but the disadvantage of difficulty in arranging frame by frame analysis. Another, rather longer approach, is for the observer to train himself up to experienced worker's performance and then analyse himself. The usual method is to concentrate on very small portions of the job per cycle and to attempt, by patient questioning of the operator, to prove or disprove hypotheses arising from this concentrated examination.

Multifarious factors make observation difficult, and these difficulties can only be overcome by an individual consideration of each problem. Some general solutions are, of course, possible. The first method is to seek to improve the study conditions by a change of factors, either by moving the operation to a more suitable position or by some similar action. The great danger of this procedure is that the true job skills may not become apparent, and the resulting training programme is then less effective. The question of operator attitudes will be dealt with later in this chapter as a general effect that concerns analysis of all the three areas, physical skills, brain skills, and job knowledge.

For the third problem area, time required to observe many cycles of an operation, a simple shorthand has been developed, based on MTM terminology, which greatly simplifies the task of recording observed manual motions. Figure 5.1 gives the short glossary required.

R	Reach	Limbs move, but do not carry any object
M	Move	Limbs move, and do carry an object
G	Grasp	
P	Position	Place or locate object carried by limb
R	Release	Release object after a position, move, or grasp

Fig. 5.1 MTM terminology

This, our experience in teaching skills analysis has shown, can be very quickly acquired by analysts and training officers.

The time taken to observe and to understand an operation is closely allied to the fifth potential difficulty, that is, observer fatigue. Many experiments, both in laboratories and in real-life situations, have demonstrated the fact that people have the power to concentrate really hard for a maximum of 20 minutes to half an hour. Analysing physical work demands a high level of concentration, so it is necessary to allow a recovery break of 5 to 10 minutes after every 30 minutes or so. By a break, we do not mean necessarily a cup of tea and a sit down, but a definite change of activity, for example, a chat with the operator, making a telephone call, writing some notes on the job, and so on. If observation is attempted continuously for, say, $1\frac{1}{2}$ hours, then it is probable that at least half the recorded data will have to be scrapped and done again because it will be unclear, out of sequence, too sketchy, or illegible. The last problem point we have mentioned is a very common one, not only in carrying out training analyses but also in most work measurement techniques. It may seem ridiculous to do so, but it is easy to skip elements, to forget the link elements at the end of one cycle and the beginning of the next, or to add non-existent elements to the analysis. The only way to avoid this is to check meticulously the completed analysis, either against the experienced operator or, more revealingly, to perform the job personally following explicitly the instructions written on the analysis sheet step by step.

To demonstrate this last point, try noting how someone uses a telephone or an adding machine, and then see if you can make the telephone or adding machine work, following word for word your notes.

The second requirement of a useful analysis is, as we have said, to record what are the primary controlling senses. Naturally, it is more difficult to observe if an operator is listening for a sound cue, or applying a certain amount of pressure, than to see manual motions. There are two basic approaches in coping with this problem. One is to ask the operator what senses he or she is using, and it is surprising the amount of insight into their job that many operators have. The other is to eliminate or to blanket a suspected sensory part, and see how this affects the task performance. In most cases, it is necessary to use a combination of the two.

In operating a large extrusion press, the key to high production speeds was to anticipate the lag in the controls and the associated air hydraulic systems. Overanticipation could damage either the product or the very expensive piece of equipment. An indication of the importance of this anticipation factor is given by the statement that every minute of scheduled time that the press was not working resulted in an irrecoverable cost of £5 ($12) per minute. It was only after intensive investigation, using questioning and elimination, that it was discovered that sound was the major sensory cue used to anticipate lag safely and effectively. The sound was of the hydraulic accumulator releasing pressure at stages during the operation cycle. It should be added that it was an extremely noisy shop and there were six accumulators scattered around. All the accumulators had their own individual pressure release sound, so that the control operator had to 'lock on' to his own particular accumulator.

The six trouble areas already listed for observing muscular movements apply with equal force to analysing and recording the control senses, but are handled in similar ways to the methods previously suggested. It is likely that any new installation of systematic operator training will begin with training for a physical skill, as in some ways this is the easiest and most natural area of training to prepare and to

50

run. It is also probably the one with the fastest payoff as described in chapters 3 and 11.

At this point, we should like to have a look at the second major area of skill which has to be analysed, that of 'brain' skills. If the analysis of muscular motions has identifiable difficulties, and analysis of the control senses has added problems, then it is clear that analysing brain skills is even more complicated at first sight than either of these. Brain skills are concerned with the activity of how people take decisions at a conceptual level rather than the more perceptual levels of manual motions. As mind readers are pretty rare animals, the problems of brain skill analysis cannot happily be left with them. The one fact that sustains the training specialist faced with this kind of dilemma is that an increasing number of people develop and use brain skills which, like most human activities, are learned in some way or other. The fact that an activity is learned means it can be taught, and thus the only question that remains is how to teach it.

Industrial applications of brain skills at non-supervisory levels are exemplified by jobs such as:

Process control operation.
Fault-finder or troubleshooter.
Qualitative inspector.
Maintenance technician.

The analysis of experienced workers in jobs such as these involves a high degree of interviewing technique on the part of the analyst, and a fair amount of comprehension of the job being analysed. Interviewing technique does not mean learning a set of rules and then applying them blindly. It is rather an ability to tune in to the operator's wavelength and to gain his confidence. Whatever happens, he is the only person who can provide the information required to produce an effective training programme. The analyst's skill lies in his ability to winkle out this information, and then record it or rewrite it in a form most suitable for training purposes. The second point, that of familiarity with the job, is very often important because in many brain skill analyses the operator is using technical or company slang terms to verbalize the way he is taking decisions.

Some of the terms used in describing surface faults on glass, ceramics, or paint finishes that we have come across include sleeks, bruises, crazes, pins, blues, orange peel, scabs, scars, edgings, blackheads, blackins, strawberries, and so on. The meanings of some of these terms are obvious, but a few are not common, although they are completely common parlance in a particular company or part of the country, or even in some cases in one department in a plant.

Brain skills are by their nature subjective, or to put it another way, two people given identical information can reach different decisions. They can organize the information in different ways depending on their previous experience, their perception of the information, their point of view, whether they have just had a rise, a row with the foreman, or whether production is breathing fire and brimstone to get a piece of plant rolling or a batch of products passed. It may be necessary for the analyst to get agreed standards written by the responsible authority, so that trainees can be trained to a common standard in order to reduce the mischievous effects of varying standards.

Synthesis

We have spent some time on the analysis of the facts required for training because, if the foundations are suspect, the whole edifice can be easily blown down however we decorate the superstructure with sophisticated training technology or glossy training centres. To continue briefly the analogy with building, the synthesis of the analysed facts is the steel frame of the building.

When thinking about the synthesis of the analysis to produce a dynamic training programme, we have to consider the function of each part of the programme. The kinds of stresses that are going to be put on the synthesis include:

Acceptability to trainees.
Speed of acquisition of the desired end behaviour.
The availability of equipment, time, and instructors.
Common skills or peculiar skills being taught.
Teaching of the correct skill.
Expense in terms of men, money, and materials.

These, and many other less concrete questions, have to be answered before it can be said that the synthesis is anywhere near perfect.

Synthesis is the recombining of the identified facts, in such a way that the learning process is optimized by feeding new information to the learner in easily digested portions, rather than asking him to spend considerable time and effort in breaking up the total task, *by himself*, into digestible bits. Even a cursory examination of this definition and reason for the procedure of synthesis reveals some of the less concrete questions we mentioned earlier. For instance, what is an 'easily digested portion'? It naturally varies according to the capacities of the learner, the instructional techniques available, the previous experience of the trainee population, the type of skill to be taught, and so on.

The key task, therefore, in deciding how to group together the analysed facts is to establish what is an 'easily digested portion'. This task is greatly assisted by the basic philosophy of skills analysis, namely, that people learn effectively when they are asked to absorb one point of difficulty at a time. To absorb a point of difficulty means to be able to perform that given point of difficulty at experienced worker's standard. Points of difficulty may be related to time, but not necessarily so. One point of difficulty can be a couple of seconds long, for example, the correct tweezer grasp of a radio valve component, or it can be several minutes long, such as learning a job sequence after having acquired the necessary manual skills.

There is one very useful rule of thumb for identifying points of difficulty in a physical skills analysis. This is: If there is difficulty in analysing a portion of the task, then there is almost certain to be one or more points of difficulty in that portion. In a shortened form, this is saying, 'if it's difficult to analyse, then it's difficult to learn'. The corollary of the statement is that care needs to be taken in the synthesis of these portions of the task, and time spent on thinking about the synthesis will be amply repaid in reduced training times.

For brain skills, no such easy rule of thumb exists so that the task of synthesis has to be tackled in a different way. The key, as always, lies in the quality of the initial analysis. If it has distilled the essence of a brain skill task through intelligent observation, questioning, and trials, then the task of synthesis is much easier. In fact, the main problem in synthesis is to decide how the brain skills are going to be taught, and for this the whole range of training technology may be used. Simulators of varying simplicity or complexity, audio-visual equipment, such as synchronized tape-slide projectors, sound film loops, concept films; programmed instruction of linear, branching, and algorithmic forms; movie films; fault-finding strategy manuals. It is not the purpose of this book to go into detailed descriptions of these training tools, but a list of references will be found in the bibliography. In addition, current developments are examined in such journals as *Industrial Training International* and many business journals.

Having digressed into the important field of training technology, we return now to synthesis, our main concern, and consider a case study.

A firm extruding thin-walled plastic tube in a variety of colours and sizes had problems of training their extrusion plant operators who worked in teams of three. The plastic was a viscous liquid pumped through an annular extrusion head around a mandrel into a setting solution. On contact with the solution, the plastic set almost instantaneously. The setting solution was black and opaque, and the extrusion head was completely submerged in it. Most adjustments affecting the final product had to be carried out with the head and mandrel submerged, and the sense of touch was vital. It was vital also because the extruded tube could easily be broken by too much pressure on it as it passed over the mandrel. The problem, therefore, was to train for a delicate job on something that could not be seen, leaning over a vat of black liquid, using spanners on invisible set screws in close proximity to an easily damaged moving product.

The analysis of both manual and brain skills was quite difficult to carry out, both skills being investigated by questioning and in the case of the physical skills, by demonstrations on 'dry land' wherever possible. The synthesis was also difficult, because the physical skills were closely interlinked with the brain skills, so that any manual motions had an immediate effect on the product of a continuous process. To summarize the results of the considerable thought that went into the synthesis, a simple rig was designed that gave the trainee the experience of leaning over and adjusting the head.

This taught the kinaesthetic sense required for location of the set screws. The next step was to make this a 'blind' location by covering the head, and the last step was to submerge the head in water so that the effects of working in a liquid could be taught and learned. We have described only a section of the training synthesis in order to demonstrate some of the approaches to analysis and synthesis, and in particular the use of a simple simulator to develop the trainee's abilities by easily absorbed steps.

This case history also illustrates the contribution that 'off the job' training can make to 'on the job' performance. A lot has been written and talked about the relative virtues of 'on the job' and 'off the job' training, and the only reason for adding to them is to examine the contribution their relative virtues can make to systematic non-supervisory training.

Our view had better be stated at the outset. From a realistic profit viewpoint, both 'on' and 'off the job' should be used in industrial training. The sole criterion as to which one or, more properly, what combination should be employed, is what proves to be most effective in training a particular set of skills. Industrial training must use whatever training technique is most economic. A selection of attributes of 'off the job' and 'on the job' can be listed as shown in Fig. 5.2. It is certainly possible to extend this list, and proponents of the two approaches may rightly say that we have omitted some important factors. However, suffice to add that even from Fig. 5.2 it is no doubt possible from your own experience to recall situations where one approach has been more appropriate than the other or, we suggest, would have been more appropriate than the other.

'On the Job'
1. Real-life situation
2. Familiarity with actual products, machines, processes
3. Economic for small numbers of trainees
4. Saves cost of special training area or equipment
5. Some production available in later stages of training
6. Quicker acceptance of trainee as group member
7. Training keeps more closely in touch with production needs
8. Material supplies to trainees easily organized
9. Induction information backed up by immediate practical experience
10. Fewer problems in transfer from trainee to experienced worker

'Off the Job'
1. Easier control and guidance of trainees
2. Avoids possible damage to expensive machines or product or trainee
3. Economic for large number of trainees
4. No interruption to production
5. Less danger of picking up bad working habits and no danger of disturbing existing workers
6. Trainees learn with equals
7. Trainee not discouraged by adverse comparisons with experienced workers' production rates
8. Few instructors required
9. Less scrap produced
10. Environment more suitable to transmission of knowledge, and use of training aids more easily organized

Fig. 5.2 Advantages of on and off the job training

The question of whether to use 'on the job' or 'off the job' training is thus not the first one that has to be answered. The one that has to be answered in the design of any training programme is: What is to be trained, and how am I going to train it most economically in my current situation?

We shall return to this question in greater detail in the following chapters, but for the moment we discuss some of the psychological

55

and social factors in training. These factors are particularly concerned with the assessment of 'the current situation' and how the design of training may be influenced by them. As with all consideration of human behaviour, it is temptingly easy to generalize and simple to act disastrously on these generalizations. Awareness of these temptations produces a reluctance to generalize or to make positive statements. A computer aided planner is reputed to have said 'the problem with industry is people'. No doubt trade unionists, personnel managers, and line managers will subscribe to this view with heartfelt feeling. So, with these reservations about acting on generalizations, we can indicate some of the social factors that affect training design.

A truism often forgotten is that training is applied to people. Some training programmes we have seen have been designed for the greater glory of the man responsible, rather than to assist people to help themselves so that they fulfil a company's needs. One of the considerations in the design of any training programme, be it management development or systematic operator training, is the target population.

A large engineering firm, having a lively training department, recruited from a population with a long tradition of agriculture. The task to be trained involved the reading of written instructions for its performance. The Personnel Department was asked to hire only people who could read and write. They suggested that the filling in of application forms at the labour office would be a sufficient test, and the training department agreed. The result was the hiring of recruits with an illiteracy level as high as 10 per cent. This was due to the fact that personnel clerks completed the application forms at a verbal interview or that literate applicants filled in forms for their friends.

Another aspect of target population is the care needed in training design when, for example, retraining older workers. Here, problems of pace of progress, of training techniques used, the introduction to new environments, and the maintenance of trainees' dignity and pride assume more importance than in, say, the training of school leavers. The work carried out by Eunice Belbin (see bibliography) is of great interest when considering the training of older workers.

What can be called the 'social geography' of the plant can have a great effect also on the way training is designed, because trainees have to work within the social nexus of the plant and not in a theoretical ideal climate or, more importantly, the climate of the training unit.

Training was being carried out successfully for female members of a team operation within a training unit. Performances at the end of 'off the job' training were completely acceptable as regards speed and quality. On introduction to the shop floor, where individual trainees were assigned to existing experienced groups, some performances dropped and personal relationships in certain cases became abrasive. This was in spite of full-time follow up by instructors and the training officer. Investigations showed that each working group had what was inelegantly called a 'head cow', and in some instances the 'head cow' had not been consulted during the preparation of the training programme, although some of her colleagues and even members of her own group had been involved. The result was social blackmail whenever an 'upstart trainee' arrived in the group. The additional consultations took place, although in the event they did not add or subtract anything to the training programme. Honour was satisfied, harmony and production performance were restored.

The case above is a shop-floor example of what is the bane of any organization chart. A written organization chart can never reveal the subtle social links and pressures that exist in real-life communities such as an industrial company. Thus, training has to be aware of the social geography of the plant in order to decide whether it will have any deleterious effect on a training programme. The other point that is worth noting about social geography is that it is rather like a political map of the world, constantly changing, in most cases slowly, but occasionally quite dramatically.

If, now, we widen our scope and include some of the broader social and psychological factors that can affect the design of training, it should become apparent that the achievement of an ideal training situation is an impossibility. If this fact does become apparent, then we shall be immensely cheered because the whole message of this book is that perfection in training can never be attained, although it is economically essential, and possible, to get closer to perfection than a number of existing training managers do.

In an era of spreading national and international communications, the influx of information and knowledge into every corner of the world has several important effects on industrial training and the design of that training.

One of the results of imparting knowledge is to arouse desires for previously unknown standards of living, material possessions, and so on. The mass reactions can be exemplified by the inflow of immigrants from the Commonwealth into the United Kingdom, where they can obtain a higher standard of living compared with their homeland situation. Another example is the trend, caused in part perhaps by increasing national awareness and pride, for Western European, United States, and Japanese industrial enterprises to set up manufacturing units all over the world instead of, as in the past, exporting completed products to the less developed countries.

The consequences for industrial training, especially at non-supervisory level, are obvious. The industrially advanced nations will continue to have, and to need, a portion of their labour force who may be ill educated, with different social customs, perhaps a different first language, living in an alien society which they do not fully understand, and which does not fully understand them. On the other side of the coin, the industrially advanced nations will have to introduce new and possibly strange skills to indigent people in less developed countries. In most cases, these skills are replicas of skills already being trained and used in the home location, as it is normal for existing proved products to be the first ones introduced for local manufacture.

The sum result of the two points made above is that national and cultural factors may assume importance in the design of training. For the training of immigrants, the language problems may be considerable and thus much thought has to be given to the means of communication of the training objectives. Time spent preparing visual, diagrammatic training aids, stress on demonstrations, use of bilingual instructors, slowing pace of instruction, repeating and overlearning important aspects such as safety and uncommon skills will almost certainly be repaid by good training performance. A short article[1] by Roy Williams of the Foundry Industry Training Committee (a Government-sponsored body under the Industrial Training act in the United Kingdom), illustrates these problems in some detail.

The pitfalls in the way of 'exporting' training programmes are similar, but have some peculiarities of their own. There is a great temptation to export, as an unedited whole, a successful training programme devised and run in the home plant. The essence of designing successful training is to define the training needs that have to be met, and it is certain that the training needs of an overseas location will not match exactly those of the home plant. For example, the use of an ordinary screwdriver or knowing in outline what an electric power tool looks like are skills common to a large proportion of the

British population. The same skills are not universally distributed in India or Africa, so it may be necessary to start training at a lower basic level than in, say, the United Kingdom. Again, the daily training hours programmed for the UK may not be applicable to other countries, especially tropical countries, where long midday breaks may be the 'norm'.

Another pitfall is the specification of materials for exercises which, though commonly available at the home location, may not be easily available in the export market. Examples of this, in our experience, are dry batteries for simple simulators, wire for special exercises, duplicating equipment for record forms, or printing proof reading exercises.

An example of the pitfalls which it is very difficult to foresee and avoid is a special exercise designed to develop spatial perception in an inspection task, which depended on coding various simple two dimensional geometrical shapes. Unfortunately, some of these shapes had religious, political, and sexual significances which could not be guessed at by a member of a western culture until they were rather embarrassingly pointed out. It was sometimes wondered what on earth the trainees thought about these depraved Westerners!

We shall end this chapter with the reminder that the design of training is affected not only by tangible items such as the quality of the analysis and synthesis carried out, but also by the intangibles of 'social geography' of the plant and geographical area such as cultural, religious, tribal, and national factors.

Reference

1 *Industrial Training International:* Vol. 3, No. 6. March 1968

6. Design of training programmes

In the previous chapter, we discussed the analysis of the various types of skill in order to learn *what* to train. In this chapter, we shall see the means by which we turn the accumulated mass of static facts into the dynamic entity of a training programme.

A training programme founded on the analysis of industrial skills, whether they be 'brain' skills or physical skills is, in essence, the selection of the best method or methods of communicating some selected facts to a specified audience. Put this way, it sounds simple and a restful exercise after the strains of analysing skills. Fortunately for our imagination's self-respect it is not. It is a creative problem solving exercise, involving trying to balance the demands of short training times and depth of understanding of training techniques against cost effectiveness: of ideal training principles against production demands. The either/or list could be extended to include many more examples of conflicting demands, but the common characteristic of all these factors is that they are difficult to quantify. It is possible to quantify, in part, most of the factors affecting the structure of training programmes but there always remains an element of chance, a section which cannot be predicted with confidence. Thus, in any decision made about training programmes, there is an element of the unknown and it is the ability to make risk-taking decisions that distinguishes the good programme designer from the merely average programme writer.

As in most risk-taking decisions, there is a certain amount of help available in the form of past experience, or of some general principles, and we shall cite some of these in this chapter. Consider again the definition of a training programme given earlier. 'The selection of the best method or methods of communicating some selected facts to a specified audience.'

Perhaps it still looks simple, but all we have to start with is 'some selected facts' which we have produced by skills analysis. Indeed, we cannot at this stage be certain that we have made the right selection, because normally we have collected too many facts and some will be discarded when training proceeds. In other words, what the analyst may suspect is a likely training problem can turn out eventually to be of very little consequence in terms of training effort. Conversely, overenthusiastic editing of instruction schedules can create severe training problems. Already, Scylla and Charybdis are looming up with their siren calls. The following case history may help to illustrate this.

Universal Products make in one of their plants a wide range of light fittings. Detailed analysis had been carried out some years ago and a lengthy training programme instituted, the time being taken in familiarizing trainees with the processes of assembling a great variety of products. The training programme produced the required results and was left untouched for some considerable time. Some years later, after investigation, the training programme was drastically cut by reducing the number of exercises and the range of products taught. The effect of this was to make large economies in training time but production line performance dropped alarmingly. Continued investigation showed that skills acquired by learning the assembly of a low volume production fitting were generally applicable to high volume production fittings, although training on one or two high volume fittings did not overspill into other high volume fittings. The final result was that 80 per cent of consumer demand for the low volume fitting was met by the training section which thus relieved production of a small batch product while still reducing training times to an acceptable level.

The problem, therefore, of selecting what facts to communicate is one that bedevils training just as much as it causes headaches in industrial relations, design specification, computer utilization, and many other branches of management activity. There are very few ground rules available for selecting the facts to be put over in industrial training, so the following list is of necessity rather brief.

1 Facts selected should be facts. This is a truism, but important to

remember as opinions, hypotheses, and biased statements can all be presented as facts.

2 The first selection is very rarely right. The selection will have to be modified in the light of actual usage.

3 It is better to select too many facts than too few, as it is easier to cut back than to add.

4 Any difficult parts of the initial analysis should be included in the training programme.

5 If it is possible to carry out a pilot training scheme, either during instructor training or with a trial batch of trainees, then this is an invaluable aid to making a good selection of facts.

The list will be added to from your own experience of the problems of marshalling facts, whether it be for industrial training, settling an industrial dispute, or arriving at a viable production programme.

Having made a selection of the facts the next point arises from our definition of a training programme: 'The selection of the best method or methods of communicating some selected facts to a specified audience.' This point is 'the selection of the best method or methods of communication'. Many excellent books and articles have been written about communication in general, and about certain aspects of communication in particular. It is not the purpose of this book to enumerate all these references, but a selected range is shown in the bibliography extending from Shannon's classic on communication theory, through Kapp's little book on the presentation of technical information, Gower's *Plain Words*, Thomas and others on *Programmed Learning*, Dale Carnegie on making friends, Cartwright and Zander on group dynamics, to how to use the telephone. There are thus many methods of communication, and it is possible to permutate any number of methods from the huge selection available. Faced with this situation, it is always a productive exercise to get down to basic principles which is, after all, one of the foundations of skills analysis.

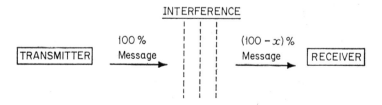

Fig. 6.1 A simple representation of communication

62

The elementary diagram shown in Fig. 6.1 is one possible representation of communication.

That this is a very simple expression of a highly complex process is not disputed, but it is occasionally useful to consider a highly complex process from an oversimplified viewpoint.

Noise is usually a problem anywhere, but in thinking about communication it is one of the two major blockages to the effective transmission of information. We shall consider the second later on in this chapter. Noise, in a communication channel, can occur for a variety of reasons, but its effect is always the same, to reduce the efficiency of transmission of information by the transmitter to the receiver. An apocryphal story from the Eighth Army's desert campaign in North Africa illustrates the point.

A faint and crackly radio message came into Montgomery's headquarters from one of the camel patrols, ranging out in the desert on reconnaissance missions. Before atmospheric noise blacked out the transmission, the base radio operator got the message, 'Send help, Rommel captured' and a position. Immediately, a brigade-size force rumbled out into the desert with banners waving and everyone very excited at the prospect of capturing the 'Desert Fox'. Cresting over a sand dune, Monty in the leading command car saw in the wadi below two British soldiers crouched in the meagre shade of their two camels but no obvious signs of Rommel. 'Where is he?' Monty barked. 'Where's 'oo?' replied the corporal. 'Rommel,' said Monty, 'you radio-ed you had captured him.' 'We radio-ed send help, camel ruptured,' answered the corporal.

The further consequences of this failure in communication are not recorded, but analagous problems can occur in industrial training.

If we examine some examples of the effects of interference on industrial training, we discover some of the remedies available, or in other words some of the methods of communication available to industrial training. They have been summarized in Fig. 6.2, but one or two additional explanations will put some flesh on the bones of the summary.

At the Urwick Management Centre, during a course for Training Officers in skills analysis, it was felt that an appreciation session on programmed instruction delivered in a straight lecture style with chalkboard assistance was not going across too well. The basic

Interference Source	Remedy or Method of Communication
External noise created by traffic or machinery	Sound proof training area. Move training area to quieter location

Too quiet speaking lecturer or poor lecturer	Use amplifying equipment
	Make groups smaller so nearer lecturer
	Change lecturer
	Put over material covered by lecturer by using:
	    Visual aids of all types
	    Programmed instruction
	    Practical demonstration
	    Individual instructor
	    Rebrief or retrain lecturer

Environment: Poor lighting
    Too hot or too cold
    Poor acoustics
    Too crowded
    Too spacious
    External interruptions, visitors, telephones, etc.
	Modify lighting
	Use projected visual aids instead of non-projected visual aids
	Improve ventilation and heating
	Reduce groups
	Partition area with curtains or panels
	Remove telephones, control visitors
	Give plenty of variety to maintain interest, short sharp sessions mixing passive and participative activities

Boredom	Variety in sessions Use of visual aids, films, filmstrips, slides, overhead projector slides, models, magnetic boards, felt boards, diagrams and wall charts, audio visual systems, programmed instruction, chalk boards Use of lectures, role playing, discussion groups, problem solving groups, special exercises, job exercises, stamina runs, demonstrations, participative activities Planned breaks, changes of pace and emphasis, occasional non-work orientated talks
Discouragement	Fast feedback of training progress Praise where due, correction when there is not fast recognition, and assistance to remedy errors or learning difficulties On to whole job as soon as possible Trainee treated as an individual and given as much individual help as possible

Fig. 6.2 Methods of communication available in industrial training

difference between linear and branching programmes was being laboured. But by putting a suitable joke into two short linear and branching programmes written on overhead projector slides, the point was made much more effectively, getting the attention of the audience and saving time at one and the same moment.

In teaching a long, two-hour cycle on complex electronic equip-

64

ment, the problem was not of the manual skills being used, but of remembering the correct assembly sequence. Charts and step by step written instructions were tried, but were not entirely successful. The key to the problem was to tape the written instructions on to a dictation machine cassette. The playback was through lightweight stethoscope earphones from a foot-controlled dictation machine, leaving the hands and eyes completely free for the task. The results amply repaid the time of preparing the tapes and the cost of the dictation equipment.

While developing the training for a particular miniature assembly operation, a fair amount of time and effort was put into the development of a delicate wire handling exercise where visual acuity, hand steadiness, and control were the key items. The actual materials used in the job were in short supply and expensive, so other simulated methods had to be used if possible. A rather complex simulator was built with several sophisticated feedback devices. It did not teach the required skills. After some further thought and trials, a sewing needle stuck in a cork which was threaded using a fine stiff piece of nylon thread was found to be ideal.

The three cases above are a sample of a very long list of available examples, where the choice of the correct way of communicating some desired information has paid back tenfold the effort spent on making the choice.

We began this discussion of communications by stating that there were two major blockages to effective communication, one being interference and the other not being mentioned. It will have become clear that so far we have talked about communication in somewhat mechanistic terms, but it is also obvious that communication generally takes place between people, indirectly in the case of this book and directly for the major portion of systematic industrial training.

Often, it has been said that industry's main problem is people; they will unfortunately make judgements and act as individuals instead of being solid, dependable, and obedient like lathes and machine tools. People will ask questions and produce ideas conflicting with your own and, further, they have the irritating habit of getting tired or even bored. Whoever heard of a lathe getting bored by the job you are asking it to do?

In industrial training, people are all too often bored or fatigued because in designing training programmes the person responsible has forgotten one of the cardinal rules of training: 'Learning is tiring.'

The task of relating new knowledge to the lessons learned from past experience is one of the most exhausting undertakings to which man can subject himself. This task is not made any easier in some instances by the way that the new knowledge is communicated, such as a 75-minute lecture with no visual aids in a stuffy room at a plant in Scotland by a quietly spoken man from Texas. However important the subject, it is certain that a large proportion of the trainees will not be able to recall the last hour of the lecture.

It is thus very important to take note of the psychological factors that can help or hinder communication. A few points to watch are:

1 Sessions on any one topic should not run for more than from 30 to 45 minutes, followed by a change of subject or activity.
2 Sessions requiring trainee participation should be interspersed with passive sessions.
3 Participative sessions should be included immediately after lunch and towards the end of the morning and afternoon periods.
4 General sessions such as company history, company products, etc. should be made as novel and as interesting as possible to act as brief breaks from concentrating on the job in hand. These sessions are a good place to try out new presentation techniques before general adoption.
5 Relate the current session or day's programme to past and future work, and if possible to the trainee's own experience. The trainee has to do this to learn anyway, so try to help him as much as possible.
6 The logical order of sessions in a training programme is very rarely the best psychological order, and it is normally better to give preference to the psychological order.
7 Vary speakers, presentation methods, and activities throughout the day in order to give variety; there is some truth in the saying that 'Variety is the spice of life'.
8 But do not overdo the variety, as the trainees will begin to wonder what or who is hitting them. From the point of view of training technique, as well as of administrative convenience and organization, it is sound policy to make one person responsible for a course, to act as anchor man and link, to whom trainees can turn at any time on either work or personal problems.

9 Give trainees a continuous and an honest feedback of their performance and they will do the same for you, so that you can make the always necessary improvements to the training programme.

When the problems of industrial training are considered, there is usually one small crumb of comfort available to the man concerned with systematic non-supervisory training and that is that it is normally possible to specify the audience to some degree.

The criteria used may be very broad; for example, all trainees may have to be females between the ages of 17 and 30, but with the development of training expertise more precise criteria can be formulated such as standards of eyesight, dexterity, spatial abilities, and so on. Matching the audience more closely to the known abilities required in order to do the task satisfactorily means that the training programme can be tailored more accurately to the needs of the trainees.

We shall expand on this point in the next chapter, which is concerned with people in training, and introduces the second part of this book. Thus, with this chapter, we complete the detailed discussion of skills analysis, and having navigated you so far without mishap we hope the rather more open seas of what to do with it now we have got it lie ahead in Part II.

Part II

7. People in training

In Part I, we considered how to assess training needs, and the way in which analysis of the mental and physical skills involved in work can lead to effective training programmes designed to meet identified needs. Training, however, is organized by people and is for people, so this chapter deals mainly with the selection, training, and development of training staff and trainees.

Training is not an end in itself, but essentially a part of the total framework of effective management. In one sense, the most important 'people in training' are the managers themselves. Indeed, there are examples of first-class training being provided by companies who employ no specialist training staff. In these companies, every manager and supervisor regards the development and training of his workers as one of his major responsibilities, and is willing to spend the necessary time and effort to obtain the results he wants. Usually, this state of affairs is found in small companies where each manager knows instinctively how important it is that the learning process should be properly organized. He may not dignify what he is doing by the title of organized training—indeed often he fails to recognize that what he is doing meets the requirements of his Industrial Training Board—but nevertheless the process is effective in that people learn their jobs well and in a reasonable time. In larger companies, managers often find difficulty in devoting the necessary time and effort to do their own training. They employ specialist training staff, either full time or part time, to help them. But the responsibility and drive required for successful training remains with managers; they cannot opt out of their role by employing specialists. This is so important a subject that we devote the whole of the next chapter to it.

Training Officers

In all companies, there is a need for an executive who acts as a focal point around which the company's training effort can be organized. In small organizations, this is often the chief executive himself. In larger companies, one manager may be designated as the 'training officer', although he only fulfils this role part time. Often, the personnel manager is also the training specialist, though in large companies a specialist training officer may be employed. In every case, there should be one man who is able to give 'training advice' and who can help to develop attitudes in other managers which enables them to provide better training in their departments. Obviously, the detailed knowledge of training techniques which this person should possess varies with the size of the company. It is ridiculous to expect a manager who is only responsible for training as one of his activities, to know as much of the detail of training techniques as would the full-time training manager in a large company. Everyone responsible for training, however, should know the basic principles of how people learn, be able to carry out a simple training needs assessment, and have sufficient background knowledge of training matters to be able to call in the right kind of assistance should the need arise. It seems to us that the Training Boards can provide a useful service in helping companies, particularly small ones, to develop one manager who understands the basic principles of training.

In writing about what a particular training specialist should know, and his background and experience before he takes up his job, there is the obvious difficulty that the size and technology of companies vary so widely. If the subject is dealt with exhaustively, as Nancy Taylor has done in her book *Selecting and Training the Training Officer*,[1] there is always the danger that the executive in a small company may regard much of the detail as irrelevant to his needs. Indeed, he would be right. However, the principles on which Mrs Taylor's book is written are relevant to all companies of whatever size, and it is up to chief executives to apply these principles to their own situation.

In appointing the manager who will act as the training specialist, it is important to remember that the man must act as a manager who possesses training expertise. It may be more convenient, therefore, to appoint a man who has proved himself as a manager, and teach him 'training' rather than to recruit a 'welfare orientated educationist' and try to develop him to act as an effective member of a modern management team. Another solution may be to appoint a young man who has received a good initial training in a specialist department, such as personnel, and give him the opportunity to act as the manager responsible for the training function. In our experience, responsibility for the training function has proved to be a good stepping-stone in the career pattern of future general managers. There is sense in this because responsibility for training, say, all non-supervisory staff, will teach a young man a great deal about the detail of how work is performed in the organization. This will be of inestimable value in his future career.

In considering the nature of the knowledge and skills which should be possessed by training officers, Nancy Taylor[2] identifies five main areas:

Company and industry or business background.
Management theory and the training function.
Background education and training knowledge.
Training methods.
The techniques of instruction.

Before the appointment is made, it is essential to define the authority, duties, and responsibility of the job as well as the salary scale. The man's relationship with other members of the firm should also be stated.[3] We do not propose to go into the detail of these matters here, other than to say that the training of a training specialist requires time and thought. There are far too many instances of training officers being appointed, sent on a short course and then expected to achieve results. This is neither fair to the man nor his company. There is far more to training than can be learned on one short course. It takes at least 6 weeks, for example, for a man to learn the essentials of skills analysis and how to apply them. A further 3 months' guidance is required before he can be expected to prepare and to run a training course for non-supervisory work with confidence and unaided.

There is one aspect of the development of the training officer as a manager which we must deal with in some detail. This is concerned with identifying his training needs on a continuing basis so that he is given every help and encouragement to improve his performance. This implies an identification of the gap between achieved and expected results, and then a decision on how to close the gap. The process can be drawn as shown in Fig. 7.1.

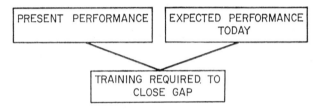

Fig. 7.1 Identification of the gap between achieved and expected results

In developing companies, it may happen that the present achievement of a satisfactory standard of performance is insufficient to meet future needs. This denotes a need for training if the current training officer is to be able to prepare efficiently to meet future requirements. This is illustrated in Fig. 7.2.

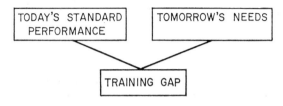

Fig. 7.2 Identification of the gap between present performance and future needs

A simple and obvious example of this kind of gap occurs when a company plans to introduce a change in its technology. The training officer may be proficient in preparing courses for traditional machine setters, but the introduction of automation or of a very advanced degree of mechanization, requires that he is able to work with control engineers, and be qualified to prepare training schemes which train ability not only to perform a specified task, but also to enable maintenance staff and process operators to work closely together as a team in keeping the plant at a maximum state of utilization. He will require, therefore, additional knowledge about a training approach for process industry and of the methods of training people to work as teams. It may not take him long to acquire this knowledge, but if the need has been recognized time will be saved later by not making the more obvious mistakes.

If training needs are to be defined clearly on this basis, two things are fundamental:

Table 7.1 PART OF A MANAGEMENT GUIDE FOR A TRAINING OFFICER

MAIN PURPOSE OF JOB: To improve the effectiveness of training programmes within the company, with the object of obtaining improved performance from non-supervisory staff.

TASK (KEY RESULT AREA)	*OBJECTIVE* (STANDARD OF PERFORMANCE)
1. *Attitude Formulation* To develop, within the company, the attitude which will contribute to the achievement of the main purpose	1. Line management and supervisors in most functions genuinely accept training as a tool of management 2. Non-supervisory staff begin to be involved in training

2. *Involvement of Training Committee*
To ensure that the overall direction of the training function is in line with company policy
	1. The training committee fully accepts and discharges responsibility for:
	  (a) Assessing company's training needs.
	  (b) Setting priorities for those who shall be trained and for the allocation of resources.
	  (c) Establishing cost budgets for training.
	  (d) Reviewing and evaluating results achieved.

3. *Apprentice Training*
To establish a systematic procedure for training maintenance department apprentices to become competent craftsmen
	1. An adequate number of apprentices to be trained on the basis of the Engineering Industry Training Board syllabus, supplemented by an analysis of skills needed on the shop floor
	2. Apprentices to be taught to achieve quality standards at experienced worker's speed for basic skills
	3. Syllabus and procedures worked out for second and subsequent year training, including maintenance of electronic equipment
	4. Procedures established so that:
	  (a) Apprentice training needs assessed on basis of skills required on shop floor.
	  (b) Cost of apprentice training is recorded.
	  (c) Results are evaluated.

4. *Training of Training Department Staff*
To develop a highly competent training force
	1. Numbers of the training department as a group:
	  (a) Understand how people learn.
	  (b) Appreciate the techniques of training and instruction.
	  (c) Know how to:
	    (i) assess training needs,
	    (ii) cost training activities,
	    (iii) evaluate results of training.
	2. Members of the training department can communicate with line managers on an effective basis and command the latters' confidence as specialist advisers

75

1 The key result areas of the training officer's job must be established.

2 Precise performance standards for each key result area must be agreed between the training officer and his superiors.

Anything less is bound to lead to 'woolly' thinking and concentration on inessentials. The key result areas do not embrace all the things a training officer can do, but only those areas which are crucial to an achievement of the main purpose of his job—in other words, the areas which have an impact on profits.

The identification of the 'areas of excellence which really have an extraordinary impact on economic performance'[4] is of itself no guarantee of results. It is also necessary to set performance standards for each key result area, 'a statement of the conditions which exist when the result is being satisfactorily achieved'.[5] A performance standard should point the way to improvement, but it should not be a statement of ideal, unattainable conditions. Where possible, standards should be quantified, and the exercise of thinking through what ought to be achieved directs attention to the action needed to achieve results. The chart in Table 7.1 is an example of the sort of thing required.

Having agreed the objectives and standards, the next step is to prepare a detailed programme for achieving them. Performance should be reviewed between the man and his boss at regular inter-

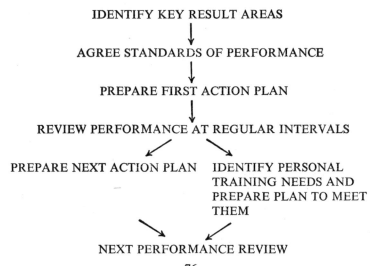

IDENTIFY KEY RESULT AREAS
↓
AGREE STANDARDS OF PERFORMANCE
↓
PREPARE FIRST ACTION PLAN
↓
REVIEW PERFORMANCE AT REGULAR INTERVALS

PREPARE NEXT ACTION PLAN   IDENTIFY PERSONAL
                                  TRAINING NEEDS AND
                                  PREPARE PLAN TO MEET
                                  THEM

NEXT PERFORMANCE REVIEW

vals. From consideration of anticipated and achieved results, not only will necessary revisions to the programme become clear, but also the training needs of the man will be identified. The development of the training officer as a person can thus take place in a planned way and his work integrated fully with his company's overall objectives, as the table on page 76 demonstrates.

This, of course, is 'management by objectives'. Although to obtain optimum results from a company's viewpoint the same process will be applied widely throughout the company, there is no reason why the training officer and his boss should not apply the principles to their own staff regardless of whether or not this approach to management is applied elsewhere in the firm. At a minimum, it will serve to concentrate on essentials and enable the training of the training officer to develop systematically. For example, using this method to identify training needs for training staff, the selection of books for guided reading, or courses for them to attend, is likely to take place in a purposeful, rather than in a haphazard manner. To quote Nancy Taylor once again:

> The relationship between key result analysis and performance review as a basis for the training officer's (OWN) training plan is an important one. Failure to recognize the significant key result areas is likely to lead to a wrong assessment of his training needs, which in turn, inevitably leads to disappointment with the company's overall training results.[6]

Instructors

The success or failure of a training scheme ultimately depends on the quality of the actual instruction given. The selection, training, and subsequent development of instructors is, therefore, of great importance. Normally, instructors are recruited from within the company. A good working principle is to ask oneself whether the man being considered is the sort of individual with which one would wish to staff the department, because his attitudes and work habits will be transmitted unavoidably to trainees. Often, this sort of person is the one who can least be spared, but it is worth making the effort and suffering the inconvenience to release him as, in the long term, the benefits will be considerable. Some form of systematic selection procedure should be employed. The basic abilities and performance capacity of possible candidates will be known from their work history within the company. Their capacity and motivation is known only in relation to

Table 7.2

PERSONAL SPECIFICATION FOR TRAINING INSTRUCTOR:
HOURLY PAID STAFF

	Job Content	*Essential*	*Desirable*
I PERSONAL DATA Age:	The age range may be wider, provided the individual has sufficient experience of the job and is mature	AGE: 20–50	When the situation permits, consideration should be given to the age of the instructor in relation to that of the trainees and should be within the likely age range of the trainees
Sex:	The sex will vary according to the industry. In general, follow the supervisory practice in the industry	SEX: As normal for supervision in the industry	
Domestic:	Marital status will be important if instruction is done in widely varying locations; otherwise it is immaterial	MARITAL STATUS: Immaterial except where mobility is required	
Rewards:	Where possible, in line with rates for supervisors in the company		
PHYSICAL FACTORS	The work is physically tiring, much of the time will be spent standing even when training in sedentary jobs	HEALTH and STAMINA: A1– but a limp is not an eliminating factor	
	An instructor must express himself clearly and lucidly and may often have to speak above noise. He must also be patient and not overbearing with trainees, but at the same time speak with authority	SPEECH: Above average clarity MANNER: Patient but firm	Able to use the operators' vernacular Able to give advice on matters beyond the work situation
		APPEARANCE: Neat and business-like. Must set an example to trainees, as he is setting the standards for the company	

78

	Job Content	Essential	Desirable
III EDUCATION and EXPERIENCE	In general, he will need to have a better basic education and technical education (or experience) than the existing operators or trainees. His understanding of the job needs to be greater than that ultimately required by his trainees. He needs the ability to perform the job consistently at a high performance level	BASIC EDUCATION: Above average of existing operators or trainees TECHNICAL EDUCATION/ EXPERIENCE: Above average for the job WORK EXPERIENCE: A record showing consistent high performance for a period equal to 3–4 training periods. Good safety, attendance, and timekeeping record	Evidence of versatility and adaptability within the operations concerned Experienced in training
IV SENSORY DISCRIM- INATION, DEXTERITY, and ACCURACY	The work involves demonstration of the correct method and results at any time it is required	Normal standards for operators	
V MENTAL REQUIREMENTS	The instructor must be able to recognize differences in trainees and their difficulties, and decide the appropriate course of action. He must be able to communicate clearly up and down the line; will be required to maintain records and to interpret them	INTELLIGENCE: Minimum 60 percentile for general population	Depends on future intentions–is he being groomed for wider responsibility?

PERSONALITY

In general, instructors are outgoing people and an indication of suitability for this job could be membership of the committee of a club or society.

A STABILITY — Emotionally stable and consistent. The stress in training can be considerable at times.

B PERSEVERANCE — Has shown ability to overcome day to day problems on his job. High frustration tolerance.

C LOYALTY — Shows more than average loyalty as an operator.

D SELF-SUFFICIENCY — Able to use discretion and to make his own decisions.

E EXTROVERT — Must be reasonably outgoing.

F GENERAL — Emotionally well balanced, well liked, and respected.

G MOTIVATION — Must have genuine interest in developing people.

79

their existing job, so there remains the problem of relating these to likely performance on the new job.

To make such an assessment of potential it is necessary, as with other jobs, to have a written description of the job requirements, and then specify the personal qualities required to fulfil them. An example is given in Table 7.2. It is then possible to determine which abilities required by the new job could not have been demonstrated while performing the old job. The emphasis of the selection process can then be directed towards a measurement, where possible, or an assessment of these. This calls for a systematic analysis and interpretation of the work history in relation to the extra abilities or personal characteristics required, and the planning of the interviews in such a way that the information obtained makes a reasonable assessment of the individual's potential and motivation possible.

Although instructors must be competent to do the job they are going to teach, it is also important that they should possess ability and skill in teaching. Above all, it is important that they should have an interest in other people and a real desire to impart knowledge to their trainees. Pieper, in his *Introduction to Thomas Aquinas*[7] puts the point well:

> (The Teacher) possesses the art of approaching his subject from the point of view of the beginner, he is able to enter into the psychological situation of one encountering a subject for the first time. There is an element in this that goes far beyond the realm of method, of didacticism, of pedagogical skill. To put it another way, in this attitude the methodological skill which can be learned is linked with something else that probably cannot ever be learned, really.

Instructors learn most by practice, rather than by listening to and absorbing the content of lectures. Although it is necessary to teach them the basics of instruction, it is desirable to take them through each part of the training course they are to teach, and to explain each detail of it. If it is possible to provide a 'pupil', so much the better. Such a 'pupil' may be a management trainee or some person who is likely to be interested as much in the technique of teaching, as in acquiring the skills involved. Once the instructor has grasped the aims and principles of the method of instruction to be used, he will no doubt be able to suggest improvements in detail.

The instructor needs to understand the principles on which skills analysis training is founded because he is likely to be accustomed to instructional methods which do not isolate difficulties, and which place most emphasis on quality at the expense of speed. Thus, he should understand the advantages of:

Teaching one point of real difficulty at a time. Once this point has been grasped, the instructor often gives considerable help in devising basic training exercises.

The value of learning each part of the job at full production speed and quality from the beginning, and how this avoids 'speeding up' in the later stages of training.

The importance of the analysis as a basis for instruction and the importance of teaching a standard method of performing the job to avoid confusion in the minds of trainees.

The reasons for building up the basic exercises into increasingly lengthy production runs, each with its target of performance.

The training of instructors is a specialized subject in itself, outside the scope of a book written primarily for line managers. However, W. D. Seymour has treated the subject more fully in his book *Industrial Training for Manual Operations*, and the interested reader is referred to this for further information.[8]

The development of instructors depends to a great extent on the coaching abilities of the training officer. Most new instructors have difficulty in seeing small deviations made by trainees in the pattern of hand movements which have been demonstrated and taught. Particularly during the early stages, the instructor must be persuaded to look for these and take remedial action. As confidence and ability develop, the instructor will suggest modifications to the detail of the training course and many can be developed to undertake analysis work unaided.

Analysts

It is likely that only the larger companies will employ analysts in their own right. Normally, the training officer will undertake his own analysis work. The selection of analysts is important, as on their work depends the structure of the training course. A personal specification for analysts employed in one large company is shown in Table 7.3. Many of them have been recruited from work study or planning departments, or are experienced craftsmen. The job of an analyst is normally a stepping-stone in a career pattern, leading possibly to becoming a training officer. Other analysts have been promoted to

Table 7.3. SKILLS ANALYST: PERSONAL SPECIFICATION

1. *Physical Makeup*
   Male or female. Preferred age 25 – 35 years. No physical defects, good eyesight, and hearing. Good appearance and bearing. Clear and confident speaker
2. *Attainments*
   Full time education to 16 years. Science or technical subject to 'O' level standard. Industrial experience such as work study, quality control, or junior supervision
3. *General Intelligence*
   Seventy percentile—somewhat above average intelligence
4. *Special Aptitudes*
   Mechanical aptitude. Spatial ability. High auditory, visual, and tactual sensitivity
5. *Interests*
   Genuine interest in the development and training of people, solving of practical rather than intellectual problems
6. *Disposition*
   Acceptable at all levels up to middle management. Self-reliant, reasonably outgoing, and dependable
7. *Circumstances*
   Willingness to travel if company units are scattered
   The job should be regarded as a stage in personal development

foremen's posts. The training of analysts should cover at least the following syllabus:

The principles of skills analysis training.

How to make analyses of mental and physical skills.

Analysing the quality aspects of work.

Structuring a training course, programme building, and devising special exercises.

Preparing training manuals.

Tactics of investigation and analysing work for training purposes.

How to make a training needs analysis.

Report writing.

Criteria for evaluating training results.

If the analyst is also to be responsible for training the instructor and monitoring the first training course, he will need to know:

The principles of good instruction.

How to train and coach instructors.

How to deal with problems likely to arise on the training course.

Trainees

The effectiveness of a training scheme obviously depends considerably on selecting the most suitable recruits as learners. Some 'wastage' is unavoidable, but the aim should be to choose candidates of an appropriate level, to arouse interest and loyalty during training, and thus ensure that the company retains their services. To achieve this aim, consideration has first to be given to: 'Can do' factors, i.e. candidates must possess a given level of intelligence and of special job aptitude. If they do not, they will generally be unable to absorb the training and successfully reach a standard of competent job performance. 'Will do' factors, i.e. candidates must want to do the job, and have the personal characteristics which will translate this desire into action.

'Can do' factors can be determined objectively by the use of selection tests, which assess an applicant's possession of the necessary aptitudes and abilities such as hand-eye co-ordination, visual acuity, reasoning ability, and so on. Such tests must, of course, be supplemented by a well-conducted interview. The interview can assess the 'will do' factors best. It should explore the applicant's educational and work history and his attainments, interests, and circumstances, so as to provide indications of personality traits and level of motivation to do the job.

If, due to shortage of labour, candidates have to be taken who fall below the standards set in the personal specification, it is important that this is noted at the time of engagement. Any specific weaknesses must then be made known to the training officer and instructor, to enable them to make appropriate modifications to the course programme. For example, if a new starter shows a lower than desirable test score for hand-eye co-ordination, extra tuition on the special

Table 7.4. MAIN HEADINGS OF A PERSONAL SPECIFICATION

I. *PERSONAL DATA*
Preferred age; sex, marital status, home circumstances
II. *PHYSIQUE*
    (a) Overall health (including disabilities incompatible with good performance) and stamina
    (b) Speech, manners, and appearance (if appropriate)
III. *KNOWLEDGE*
    (a) Basic education (essential and preferred)
    (b) Technical training (essential and preferred)
    (c) Work experience (essential and preferred)
IV. *SENSORY DISCRIMINATION*
Level of vision, hearing, touch, etc., required for job
V. *MENTAL REQUIREMENTS*
Any general or special aptitudes required for good performance
VI. *DEXTERITY AND CO-ORDINATION*
Speed, accuracy, and co-ordination of movement
VII. *CHARACTER TRAITS*
Special traits required by the particular job, rather than the common traits (such as loyalty and stability) required by most jobs
VIII. *OTHER REQUIREMENTS*
Union membership; licences, etc.

exercises designed to develop this particular aptitude would be necessary.

The personal specification can be built up by considering the analysis. Table 7.4 shows the main headings under which a personal specification should be built up.

The Manager and his Training Staff and Trainees

As we have stressed constantly, a manager cannot opt out of his responsibility for the training staff and trainees. He must display a continuing interest in their motivation and progress. His main concern must be to ensure that the work of the training section is integrated with the objectives of his own department and that the trainees meet his requirements. These aims cannot be achieved if he remains aloof, and his display of personal interest can contribute greatly to the success of the training being given. Foremost among his responsibilities in this respect is to feed back to training staff information of the extent to which their work assists him in attaining his objectives. If he feels that trainees are not being taught the correct things, or fail to achieve the necessary standards, he should say so, and discuss suitable modifications to the training scheme. This sounds obvious, but it is amazing how often managers stand aside and criticize, without discussing their criticisms with training staff.

We have carried out more than one survey where managers have been asked about the quality of training given in a training centre. 'Awful' or worse, has been the reply. Asked whether they have discussed their criticisms with training staff, they have said, 'No—it is not our responsibility.'

It is helpful if the manager takes the trouble to meet his trainees throughout the training course. This eases the problem of transfer, because trainees then can judge and accept the man for whom they are going to work. Where this is not done, the trainees have been known to compare their 'new' supervisor unfavourably with their instructor. Apart from these regular visits throughout training, supervisors and managers can supplement the training usefully by talking to trainees, in a training session, about those aspects of work which they consider important.

The teaching of self-discipline is an important part of the training process. Good timekeeping, tidiness, and a pride in work should all be stressed, though the personal example of the instructor is probably of more value than repeated admonition. Managers, however, should not be surprised to hear laughter from the training section. Learning is hard work if properly organized, and trainees need relief. One form of achieving this is spontaneous laughter. This aspect of the hard work required to learn is important and is often underestimated. It is much less tiring to continue to apply what one has learnt than to learn it in the first place. For this reason, learners need rest. Normally, they take this 'on the job', but where the training has been carefully structured so that learning takes place throughout the day, breaks have to be built in to the training programme. Managers should recognize this need for 'rest pauses' because, particularly in the early stages, 'learning' is more strenuous than actually performing a job when one is 'skilled'. There have been instances where trainees have not been allowed necessary breaks because they do not happen to coincide with ordinary departmental routines. This is a mistaken policy, because the only result is that the learners take their rest when they should be concentrating on learning. The appearance of work has been substituted for real effort at learning. Naturally, the need for rest pauses decreases as the training programme progresses, so that by the time transfer takes place the trainees are working in line with normal departmental procedures.

Rates of pay and status of instructors are clearly of importance. Practice varies widely on these matters. In some companies, instructors have the same status and conditions as foremen, in others they receive less than the highest paid group of operators carrying out the job which they are instructing. There can be no hard and fast rules, but the following may be of help:

The starting rate for a new instructor should leave a margin for increase after successful performance in the job after, say, 6 months to a year.
The instructor should never lose by accepting the job. This only serves to decrease the status of what is obviously an important job. If the man has been on piecework or high overtime, the average of his last 4 weeks' earnings is often considered a good starting-point.
In general terms, an experienced instructor is likely to be of as much worth to his company as a supervisor responsible for a section comparable in size with the training centre. This assumes, of course, that the supervisor and instructor are concerned with jobs of an equivalent order of importance.

If these principles are followed, it is unlikely that a manager will fall into the trap of appointing as an instructor a person for whom he has no other job.

Payment to trainees presents less of a problem. As training continues until experienced worker's standard is attained, it is clearly inequitable to pay training rate throughout the learning process if this is more than, say, 6 to 8 weeks. If piecework is normally paid, trainees should receive any earnings due to them if they have produced more, over a period of a week, than is required by the fallback rate. It is important, however, to ensure adherence to the training programme. The increase of earnings should be planned and progressive. Some companies make special once for all payments to trainees at 'landmark' stages of the training, as, for example, achievement of the first full cycle at experienced worker's standard. Whatever payment system is adopted, it is necessary that it is felt to be fair by trainees, and gives the necessary incentive for continued improvement.

We have been considering the selection, training, and development of people in training—training staff and trainees. The welding of the performance of these people into the framework of the company is one of the most important tasks of a manager. This is the subject matter of the next chapter.

References

1 *Selecting and Training the Training Officer:* A. L. T. Taylor, Institute of Personnel Management, 1966.
2 Ibid. p. 22 et seq.
3 Ibid. p. 31 et seq.
4 'Managing for Business Effectiveness': P. F. Drucker, *Harvard Business Review*, May/June 1963, pp. 53–60.
5 *Improving Management Performance:* J. W. Humble, British Institute of Management, 1965.
6 *Selecting and Training the Training Officer:* A. L. T. Taylor, Institute of Personnel Management, 1966.
7 *Introduction to Thomas Aquinas:* Josef Pieper, Faber & Faber, 1962.
8 *Industrial Training for Manual Operations:* W. D. Seymour, Pitman, 1954.

Part III

8. Management and training

In December 1908, H. L. Gantt, one of the pioneers of modern management thinking, read a paper to the American Society of Mechanical Engineers which he called 'Training Workmen in Habits of Industry and Co-operation'. This paper represents one of the milestones of the development of management thinking. For centuries, employers had assumed formal responsibility for training craftsmen by the guild and apprenticeship system, but Gantt was stating a case for formalizing the training of the countless new types of industrial worker who had emerged from the industrial revolution. These men, untutored and largely unorganized, were required to learn their jobs as best they might. They were regarded, almost literally, as so many 'hands', selling their labour to anyone who had a vacancy. Gantt, once employed as assistant to the chief engineer at the Midvale Steel Company, was strongly influenced by his chief's thinking. This man was none other than F. W. Taylor who was already recognizing that 'ignorance on the part of management as to what men would and should produce',[1] was acting as a brake on the expansion of industrial production which would lead to higher living standards for all.

These early pioneers were preaching a lesson which is still not fully understood or accepted. It is that management has a major responsibility for ensuring that the human resources it employs are given the best help and guidance available to ensure that people can learn and perform their tasks for their own, their company's, and society's benefit. Training is thus a mainstream, not a fringe activity. It is a major responsibility of line management, not a welfare service provided by forward-looking companies.

Managers at all levels, from executive directors to supervisors, employ others to assist them in carrying out their responsibilities. The Glacier Metal Company lays down as a policy about the work of a manager: 'A manager shall appoint, train and maintain at his immediate command, a team of subordinates who are competent to carry out the work he requires of them.'[2]

The operative word is 'train'. For, if a manager does not adequately and positively instruct his subordinates in their duties and skills, how can he reasonably expect them to achieve the results he requires?

A large international American company built a new plant in Europe. Most of its personnel were hired in the local market. They are mainly concerned with process operations and plant maintenance. The company, internationally, has a large training staff and allocates substantial sums each year for 'training'. In its new plant, various efforts at training were made from the beginning. However, many of these were inadequately planned and poorly executed so that after 2 years of operation the work force at all levels was so inexperienced that almost a complete training job still remained to be done. A new general manager was appointed, who recognized that the rapid development of effective training was absolutely vital to the success of the business.

Alan Paine Ltd. are manufacturers of high quality men's knitwear in Britain. The company is expanding rapidly, and in 1966 it faced a projected increase in turnover of 25 per cent. Threequarters of this production was exported, so that it was imperative to ensure that production capacity was available to meet the increase, for export orders depend on meeting delivery dates. A new branch factory was opened in South Wales where the traditional skills associated with the hosiery industry do not exist. Using traditional training methods, it was anticipated that girls would reach target levels of production and quality in one year. Paine's could not wait that long, and the managing director laid down that skills analysis training methods should be used so that new girls would achieve the required standards in 10 weeks. Not only were the export orders completed on time, but the substantial reduction in training time obviously had a beneficial effect upon costs.

The interesting point about these two cases lies in the contrasting approach of management to training. The large corporation had the training resources and applied it in a highly traditional manner. Little real analysis of need was undertaken and the training programmes were largely irrelevant to the work situation. The smaller company had little formal training resource, but, correctly identifying a major training need, deployed the latest and most up-to-date methods to meet it.

Training Policy

Formalizing the training policy of a company helps to ensure that training effort is directed into economic channels. It is part of the process of keeping training a mainstream line activity. Many managements, interested in training and often spending large sums on training departments, are content for 'training' to exist without formulating and examining critically the results expected. There are many demands on the financial resources of a company. Some managers wish to install a computer; others to re-equip a machine shop; the marketing director wishes to enlarge the advertising budget; the research director insists that more resources are made available to develop new products. Training expenditure is thus only one item among many jostling for money. When considering claims for, say, the new machine-shop, most managements insist on some form of statement to indicate return on investment. Curiously, the same standards are seldom demanded for proposed expenditure on training. In chapter 3, we discussed how these standards can be developed. The allocation of training resources in a planned manner inevitably leads to the formulation of a training policy to answer the question, 'What are we trying to achieve for our money?'

The Perkins Engine Company of Peterborough, England, manufacture diesel engines. For many years, this company with world-wide interests has taken training seriously, but in common with most companies in the motor-car industry, training for jobs on the shop floor was mainly concentrated on apprentice training. In 1964, a reorganization of some manufacturing facilities took place. One of the changes involved the removal of the gear production shop to a branch factory in another part of Peterborough. The manager in charge of this factory recognized the important part training must play if the revised production schedules for gears were to be met. Most of the existing machines moved across during the change, but the opportunity was taken to retrain the existing setters to a higher standard of competence and to train three new setters. The training was based on skills analysis and took place on the shop floor over 6 months. It was achieved by sending two of the best supervisors to act as instructors. One automatic lathe and one hobber were taken out of production full time despite a difficult production situation.

This represented the main training effort, but the manager insisted that a part of each week during the 6 months should be devoted to training. He laid down that whenever a machine was not being used, even for 2 hours, the resident instructor (an assistant foreman) would train one or two machine setters on it. This training was based on skills analysis and, as there were thirty-six different types of machine and fourteen setters, only a sustained and purposeful programme could have achieved results in the period. The manager's determination to train was all the more remarkable as he was beset with the normal production troubles associated with opening a new department.

The results were impressive. A 16 per cent increase in productivity was recorded, partly due to new machinery, and partly resulting from training in how to work the old machinery better and the new machinery well. The number of setters required after the training programme had been completed was reduced by two, and the two additional setters needed in theory, on work study standards, to meet the increased production programme were never required. Thus, there was an effective saving of four setters who were available for work elsewhere in the company.

Other managers in Perkins took a great interest in the results of training in the gear section. They also asked the training department to help them build up skills analysis courses for their departments. At this stage, the general manager formed a training committee consisting of departmental managers and training specialists. Its purpose was to allocate resources to training and plan their use by the training staff. Although the company had a general statement of corporate training policy, the need for a formal, specific, statement of company operator training practice soon emerged. This is shown in full in the appendix to this chapter. (See page 102.) Four of its provisions were:

Training is the responsibility of line management.
Training programmes are designed and implemented to improve job performance for defined needs.
Training programmes will be based on the skills and knowledge required by experienced workers as revealed by some form of analysis.

An evaluation study to determine the effectiveness of training will be an integral part of all training programmes.

Here we have a classic situation. A company with an established, but traditional, training function tries out a revised training method in a limited area. The results are encouraging, and management formalizes its approach so that new training ideas can be incorporated rapidly and effectively into the total production situation.

Organization

Successful training depends as much on organization as on techniques. W. D. Seymour, one of the pioneers of skills analysis training, has often stated that 'training is a team job'.[3] The chart in Fig. 8.1 indicates the roles played by various members of the management team in ensuring that shop floor training is successful.

Line Management

The role of line management, is, of course, crucial. Unless they wish or recognize a need to improve training, all the representations of training staff will be to no avail.

A company in the food industry used T.W.I. training for many years. This was well organized, and had reduced training times on one key packaging line from 9 months to 12 weeks. Nevertheless, because of the seasonal nature of the work and of the latent difficulties in the task, labour turnover was high and at times production was seriously hindered because of a lack of skilled operators. The senior training staff in the company were convinced skills analysis had something to offer. The manager of the factory concerned was unconvinced but reluctantly allowed the training staff to try out an experimental course. No proper facilities or backing were provided, and although the revised training showed some marginal improvement the factory manager called skills analysis training a failure. His problem of a lack of skilled operators remains.

The lesson is simple: do a job properly or not at all. The original training was fair—it would have been excellent if management had really wished to improve it.

The follow-up of trainees after a formal training course is a critical responsibility of supervision. When follow-up is well done, the learner

Fig. 8.1 The parts played by various managers in successful shop floor training

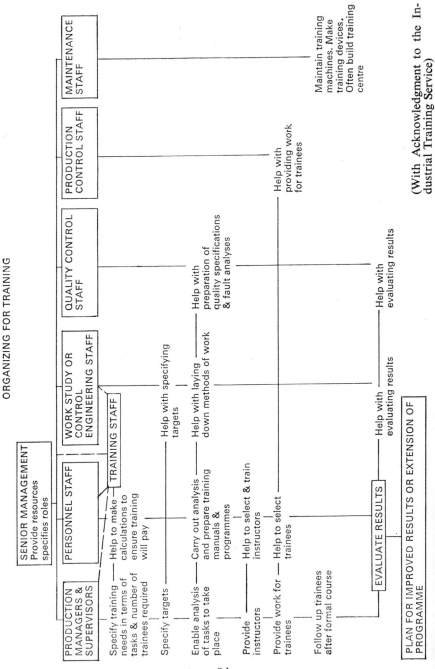

ORGANIZING FOR TRAINING

94

(With Acknowledgment to the Industrial Training Service)

receives help and encouragement and a carefully phased programme of 'new work' not seen before. Follow-up is inadequate when the trainee arrives from the training section and is assumed to have learned enough to fend for himself.

In a cotton spinning mill, a skills analysis based course for jack frame tenters reduced learning times from 1 year to 3 months. The first trainees from the training centre arrived in the production department full of enthusiasm and confident of their ability to do a good job. At the end of the first week, their production was only 75 per cent of target and the girls were dispirited. Close observation by training staff showed that their skills and quality had not deteriorated. The trouble lay in the fact that the foreman had placed the girls on machines which were inadequately serviced and on which his older girls refused to work.

Work Study

The relationship between work study and training can be summed up in the phrase 'work study states *what* should be done, skills analysis teaches *how* the what is to be achieved'. The question is often asked whether it is the job of the skills analyst to alter methods. We believe the answer is 'no'. Undoubtedly his analysis will highlight areas where methods improvement can take place, but his proper course is to bring these to the attention of the work study department and production management, not to introduce unilaterally new working methods in the training section. The work study department will also provide information about the experienced worker's standard which all learners must attain before their training can be regarded as complete. Close liaison between the work study and training departments is essential—each has much to contribute to the other's success.

In a garment factory the work study officer was given responsibility for introducing systematic training. This lady was first trained in skills analysis and applied it to good effect in reducing the training times, for sewing machinists, from 18 months to 4 months. As a result of her detailed analysis work, and in her role as the work study officer, she was able to suggest to line management minor, but significant alterations in working methods. Like other work study practitioners of our acquaintance, she stated that the close analysis required for training had given her a deeper insight into the tasks performed by operatives, and to that extent had improved her work study practice.

Control Engineering

The role of control engineering staff in relation to training in process and automated industries is perhaps less well understood. The task of operating staff in a modern man/machine system is to close the loop. That is to perform duties or routines not performed automatically, to monitor the system, and make adjustments not made by machine controls. This means that the operator must know exactly what the machine mechanisms will, and will not, do. It is the control engineer's job to ensure that the process is under control, to know how it works, to understand the meaning of deviations from the norm, and to be able to return the process, if it has deviated, to a static state. But the control engineer will expect process operators to be in daily attendance at the machine. If they are to be able to perform properly, the information on which they will make decisions must come from the control engineer. He has the requisite knowledge and plays, therefore, a vital part in the analysis of the skills required by operators. Unless he can tell them, by systematic training, how to carry out their duties, the operator will be at a loss when the unexpected happens.

British Rail built a series of semi-automatic marshalling yards. One of the main features of these yards was that a train load of wagons could be pushed over a hump and the wagons sorted into correct sidings with minimal human interference.

The main task of the operator was to select suitable leaving speeds from a braking mechanism so that each wagon rolled to its correct position in a predetermined siding. The operator based his decision on the following factors:

1 Weight of the wagon.
2 How well it ran along the rails (rollability).
3 Curvature (if any) of the siding.
4 Whether the rails were wet or dry.
5 Wind direction.
6 Fullness of the siding.

Of these factors, information on one and two was given to him by electronic equipment as each wagon approached the final braking point. Factor three had to be remembered, and factors four, five, and six were observed through a window. It was found that, in practice, operators tended to base their judgements mainly on factors three, four, five, and six and to guess factors one and two. In other words, they tended to ignore the information of the electronic equipment.

Unfortunately, the operator's guess was not often accurate, which led to a low operating efficiency. Detailed tests showed that the electronic equipment was not attaining as high an accuracy as had been expected, and that the major reason operators did not use the readings was that on several occasions their 'correct' reaction to a faulty reading had led to mishaps. Studies also showed that the equipment was 80 per cent accurate, while operators' judgements were only 50 per cent correct. The operators were then trained to use only the electronic readings as a basis for decision on the first two factors. It was explained that only 80 per cent success was expected and this was in fact achieved.

The moral of this story is that if a process is not fully under control, because of factors outside an operator's control, then it is useless to expect the operator to achieve a higher rate of success than the machinery is capable of giving. The role of the control engineer is to help the training analyst, by explaining exactly how an operator should react in order to achieve correct performance, within the limitations imposed by the process itself.

Quality Control

The role of quality control staff is obvious, but requires clarification in one respect. The written down standards of quality required at each stage of production are often unrealistic in terms of what will, and will not, pass. This means that trainees may be trained to a higher quality standard than that demanded on the shop floor. The result is nearly always confusion in the trainee's mind, and poor quality while he is learning the real acceptance limits.

In a factory making batteries, quality control had specified quality acceptance standards, in writing, for one stage of the process. Investigation showed that these written standards were so high that normal required production outputs could not be achieved. Unknown to senior management, the shop foreman and local quality control staff had devised unofficial lower standards of quality, which had aroused no comment. A skills analysis training programme was based on these lower standards and the unrealistic standards formally withdrawn.

The Foreman

It is not surprising that the role of the foreman in industry has appeared to change with the more widespread acceptance of 'scientific management'. Originally the undisputed link between management and men, he was the real 'boss' who hired and fired, planned and distributed work, and paid wages. The introduction of 'specialists' to help him has apparently, but not in fact, diminished his shop-floor leadership role. Until recently, few specialists, with power and top management backing, were available to help the foreman train his workers more effectively. However well or badly (in a specialist's opinion) shop-floor training was undertaken, undoubtedly the vast majority of foremen recognized their inescapable responsibility for teaching the starter his job. Instinctively, many of them organized this on the job training quite well. The 'Nellies' to whom the new employees were given were often natural teachers with a real interest in helping others to acquire their own skills and knowledge. At a time when on the job training is, wrongly, condemned out of hand, it is important to remember that some of it has been and will continue to be very effective.

Colin J. Brook & Co. Ltd. is a small engineering company in Northern Ireland. The total labour force is thirty-six, and management quickly recognized a need to train its own craftsmen. The company is too small to be able to equip an off the job training area or to pay wages for unproductive work. Ten apprentices were recruited and placed on carefully chosen production work from the beginning. The managing director lays down the syllabus of training while the foreman, who has been sent on an instructors' course, assumes personal responsibility for showing how each job should be done and the quality standards expected. Regular tests are given to measure progress, and the apprentices attend lectures in their own time in the evenings. Some of the lectures are given by the older apprentices who have been given the opportunity of visiting a client company to learn some specific aspect not covered by the range of work available in their own company. The use of apprentices as 'teachers' arouses interest, gives the student the benefit of learning by teaching, and helps to build up a reservoir of talent for future instructors. In many ways, this on the job apprentice training scheme breaks all the 'rules'. But the basic principles of good training procedure are present—planned sequence of practice, positive instruction, and regular measuring of results. The analysis of skills has not been undertaken formally, but the foreman is of a calibre to teach them well, and though formal analysis might well reduce training times, the capital cost of doing this is beyond the means of such a small company.

Results are what count and these are impressive. The apprentices in the machine, fitting, and welding sheet metal sections all produce reliable work and the chief draughtsman, inspector, and sales and liaison engineer were all apprentices two years ago.

The foreman must be given credit for this, and training specialists will do well to remember that a good foreman will still feel responsible for ensuring his workers are capable of meeting the standards he lays down. In the light of much unhappy experience, when other specialists were fighting for a place in the sun at the expense of the foreman, the training officer must be very careful not to let the foreman feel that training is not now one of his major responsibilities. These responsibilities include a major say in the syllabus of training to be given, the provision of instructors, the provision of work for trainees, and most importantly, the follow-up of starters after systematic training has been given.

Reads Limited, manufacturers of cans, had a considerable problem of training bodymaker mechanics. New mechanics were placed with the most experienced man in the section, but because the work was extremely complex, and no adequate training analysis had been undertaken, training was not effective. The department manager had chosen the most natural 'teacher' to look after starters. During the analysis period of building up a systematic training course, he seconded this man to help the training specialists. He did this at considerable inconvenience to himself, because he recognized the importance of improving the quality of training. On completion of the training, he took a personal interest in the follow-up of the trainees. The manager's interest in, and acceptance of responsibility, for making the training effective paid off. Improved training enabled him to achieve the same output even after considerable reduction in overtime and third shift working.

'Selling' Training to Working Groups

The importance of this aspect of training should never be underestimated. In effect, the skills analyst is asking workers to tell him in detail all the minutiae of their working practices—the skills for which they get paid. It is a tribute to the responsibility of workers that invariably they are willing to do so, and so seldom make any formal demand that management will not use the information to adjust their wages.

> The loom mechanics in a cotton weaving mill were dissatisfied with the training given to loom apprentices. They demanded a better training scheme. After the details of what a skills analysis based scheme would involve had been explained, they only agreed to its introduction provided that they, and not management, carried out the analysis. The Cotton Board Productivity Centre, after getting the co-operation of both the Overlookers Association and the Employers Association, provided the training analyst, and the skills of loom 'overlooking' were analysed over a period of 6 months. This was done on the job, and the details of the analysis were discussed with the overlookers as a group in their breaks and in the evenings after work. At every stage, the overlookers felt identified with the buildup of the training scheme and were proud of the achievement of markedly reducing the traditional training time.

The way in which necessary co-operation can be obtained will vary with each company. Obviously, the past record of industrial relations and the traditional way in which communication takes place between management and workforce, will influence how operator willingness to be analysed is gained. This personal involvement of operators helps to improve industrial relations, and can assist in eradicating the latent hostility which so often exists between management and managed.

Training Committees

It will be clear that good communications, up as well as down the company structure, are as important in relation to operator and craft training as they are for other management activities. Each company knows the best way in which it can ensure that its communications are adequate, but a number have found that the formation of a training committee is of value. These committees normally fall into one of two categories. Either they are management policy forming committees, or there is more general representation including members from the shop floor.

The Perkins Engine Company Manufacturing Division's training committee, already referred to, is strictly a management committee dealing with training. The objectives for the training department are set for the year ahead, together with the allocation of adequate resources. It is expected that quantified results will be reported, and major deviations from plan are unlikely to take place without reference to the committee. In this way, training becomes an integrated management activity with supervisors recognizing clearly that they still have major training responsibilities. Information about training and discussions on the subject are held regularly with the Trade Unions, but these are handled through the regular and effective industrial relations channels.

Johnson Radley Limited set up a more broadly based training committee. This company employs a high proportion of skilled craftsmen engaged in high precision engineering work. Management proposed to introduce a skills analysis based first year engineering apprentice training course, which involved a considerable break from traditional first year apprenticeship training. The training committee comprised not only management members, but also the apprentice instructors and skilled men from the shop floor. Management used the committee not only to give information on its intentions, but also to arouse active interest and participation by its skilled workers in the preparation of a new and more effective training scheme for apprentices. These aims were achieved, in that the training analysts received wholehearted co-operation and many useful suggestions, from the skilled craftsmen. Another interesting point was that the six shop floor supervisors took it in turns to be present at committee meetings. In this way, not only did they learn what was going on, but they demonstrated their interest in training. There was also a representative from another branch of the company in the same district; the purpose of his presence was to pave the way for introducing systematic training in that branch at a later date.

We have seen how training, to be effective, must be an integral part of normal management activity. We are now in a position to discuss the role of the executive responsible for ensuring that the best specialist training, advice, and help are given to his management colleagues.

References

1 *The Making of Scientific Management:* Urwick and Brech, Volume 1.
2 *Exploration in Management:* Wilfred Brown. Heinemann, 1960.
3 *Skills Analysis Training:* W. D. Seymour, Pitman, 1968.

Appendix

Perkins Engine Company Manufacturing Division
Proposed Operator Training Practice
for Discussion at Training Committee Meeting

1 Training is the responsibility of line management.
  The group employee resourcing department offers a staff service to:

  Assist in the identification of training needs.
  Ensure that the latest training techniques and methods are available to line management.
  Assist in the selection and training of instructors.
  Ensure that the company obtains the maximum grant under the Industrial Training Act.

2 Training programmes are designed and implemented to improve job performance for defined needs.
3 Training programmes will be based on the skills and knowledge required by experienced workers as revealed by some form of analysis.
4 An evaluation study to determine the effectiveness of training will be an integral part of all training programmes.
5 All operators should receive systematic controlled training on transfer to a new position either on a basic course or on the job. Training will be in the form of basic courses where large scale needs are revealed followed by specific 'on the job' training.
6 Where a basic course and/or on the job training is available, operators will not normally be upgraded unless they have com-

pleted the appropriate course and achieved predetermined standards of performance.

7 All instructors will be selected to ensure they possess suitable qualities, and will receive systematic training in the techniques of instruction.

9. The role of the training manager

In the last chapter, we stressed the crucial role played by line management in training. As managers exist only because they have more responsibility than they can discharge personally, training their subordinates must be a mainstream activity if they are to have any real hope of achieving the results they want, through the effort and abilities of those under their command. The question is not, therefore, whether or not to train—but how well the training is to be organized.

It is often not appreciated sufficiently that training is in reality encouraging others to do what one wants them to in a work situation. Only a part of training is concerned with formal instruction; real results in application come from the way in which the 'boss' sets a good example, and builds on any formal training already given. The 'old-fashioned' foreman who was asked how long it took to train centre lathe turners appreciated this point when he replied, 'Well, most of them arrive with the skills I require, but it takes a month or two to get them into my way of thinking.'

The training manager has little part to play in this on the job follow-up process, but he can make a major contribution in improving the quality of the basic training of skills on which line management can build. There is a case in every company for a senior manager to spend part of his time ensuring that training for skill is given in the best and cheapest way possible. In most medium-sized and large companies, this role will be filled by an individual who may be titled 'Training Manager'. His job is to advise and to persuade management on how basic training costs can be reduced. He will often organize this training himself, though he had better be careful to ensure that the results of the training he achieves accord with management's real needs. His presence on the payroll is justified only to the extent to which he relieves line management of the necessity of carrying out the detailed work needed to reduce overall training costs. If he is to have the necessary influence, three prerequisites must be present:

1 As a person, his competence as a manager, and on management matters, should be such that he can contribute to general management discussions as well as to discussions on training.
2 His expertise on training matters must be sufficient to meet the needs of his company.
3 His status, earned from the above, will be as a senior manager.

Status on its own is not enough. Management ability must also be present.

In a large engineering works the personnel director was also responsible for training. Personnel practices were not very advanced and systematic training was virtually non-existent. A new works director recognized the need to improve training, and asked the personnel director to treat the matter as one of urgency. All the necessary ingredients for success were present: senior line management drive behind training; status for the man responsible for carrying it through.

One vital thing was missing. The fact that the personnel director knew so little about 'management' that he was unable to make training proposals which line managers could recognize as having relevance to their real needs. Training to him was a welfare activity, not a cost reduction process.

Too many training managers bemoan the lack of interest shown by line management in their activities, though many of them have drive, enthusiasm, and real training ability.

As consultants, we often see beautifully produced training manuals. In answer to the question, 'And what results are you getting?' too frequently we hear, 'Well, line management doesn't seem really interested in our work.'

A training manager must, therefore, be effective. What makes an effective manager? Peter Drucker in *The Effective Executive*[1] lists five ingredients present in an effective executive. They are equally true for training managers.

105

1 He knows where his time goes and he organizes himself so that he has time to think.

The training manager has many demands on his time. There are important things he must do and there are constant interruptions, but unless he makes time to think out and plan where he is going, much of his training will be ineffective. He will start focusing on things which do not matter; training activities which may look well on paper, but do not contribute to profit. His life will be one of missed opportunities.

2 He focuses on outward contribution. He asks himself 'What results are expected of me?', rather than working hard at producing training schemes which may have no relevance to the real problems of his customers—line management.

A company introduced a new product. There were considerable difficulties of design, and the labour force was completely untrained. The sales demand for the product was assured; the problem was to build up production quickly enough. During the first six months of the product's life production was meagre, and the problems of rectification, product design, and rapid buildup of operator skill seemed insoluble. A training officer was engaged, and he recognized immediately that his major task was not to produce a model training scheme for the department, but to raise skill levels rapidly so that flow of completed goods to customers would increase rapidly. Therefore, he trained six workers to analyse skills. He supervised their work, devised training exercises with them, and used them to instruct the next batch of new recruits. Though the principles of skills analysis training were observed, most of the training was done on the job, working to a hastily devised syllabus with inadequate resources. However, the flow of completed saleable work increased rapidly and line management has authorized him to spend money on refining his training scheme so that new employees can receive more sophisticated and better training.

3 He builds on strengths. He doesn't try to do the impossible or 'theoretically' correct. He looks for strengths in his colleagues, subordinates, and himself: he focuses on these and uses them to achieve results.

A training manager in a large company controlled fourteen skills analysts. One of them was relatively unsuccessful. He seemed unable to achieve results in the work he was given. The training manager recognized that he was interested in the training of inspectors, and could not be bothered with the detailed work involved in assembly operations. Furthermore, he was respected by the inspectors in the factory. The training manager, therefore, set him the task of devising a training scheme for inspectors and left him to it. The analyst worked hard and effectively, and displayed an interest he had previously lacked. That man not only improved the training of inspectors, but was responsible for suggesting major advances in shop-floor inspection procedures.

4 He concentrates on the few major areas where superior performance will produce outstanding results.

5 He makes effective decisions . . . what is needed are few, but fundamental decisions. What is needed is the right strategy rather than razzle-dazzle tactics.

These five ingredients for a successful training manager are, of course, interlinked. Every training manager should ask himself this question. 'With the limited resources at my disposal, how can I make the most effective contribution to the profitability of my organiztion?' If he follows the advice contained in Peter Drucker's book, he will find soon that any difficulties he has had in gaining line management interest will soon disappear. The implication is that he should regard himself as a manager first and a training specialist second.

A training manager's competence as a manager assumes even more importance in automated industries where the numbers requiring training are relatively few in relation to invested capital. He needs to understand the roles played by engineers and control engineers, and to be able to work closely with them. Unfortunately, the important part played by human beings in man/machine systems is often insufficiently recognized. There is sometimes a distressing tendency to assume that new or improved control systems will, of themselves, ensure that a process runs smoothly. In practice, machines are made by men and somewhere men are needed to ensure they function properly. In continuous flow production plants, operators require control skills to optimize production. As Crossman[2] has pointed out, 'oddly enough the operator can sometimes achieve better results than the engineer'. The training manager is often the person who can convince the technical specialists responsible for automated equipment that systematic training has a major contribution to make in reducing downtime and so raising productivity. He will only do so if he sees the problem as a production problem and not merely an area where training, in principle, would be a good thing.

British Rail built a number of new marshalling yards. The main feature of difference was that wagons were automatically shunted to the correct siding, so that point switching and braking of each wagon were largely performed automatically. Operators were still required to monitor the process, and make certain decisions regarding the amount of braking to be applied to each wagon. Training staff were asked to prepare a training course for the operators on this new equipment. Early on, they asked management, 'What are the criteria by which we can judge the effectiveness of our training?' The answer, 'The number of wagons shunted each shift.' Fortunately, the training staff worked closely with railway specialists and later it became apparent that the real criterion of an efficient yard was not how many wagons were shunted each shift, but rather how many wagons arriving at the yard caught the next train scheduled out of the yard to their destination. This put a new light on training priorities. It was still important to train the operators of the equipment; it was much more important to train the control staff responsible for deciding the order in which trains should be dealt with on arrival at the reception sidings.

If the training manager is to focus his attention on profit earning areas of work, he needs to train himself to identify them. We have referred in chapter 7 to the utility of a 'management by objectives' approach in training and developing training managers. In thinking about his job, every training manager can use this approach to develop guide lines for effective action. We have already stressed that it is not enough for him to be a training expert. He also has responsibility as a manager in four main areas:

1 Forecasting and planning.
2 Budgeting and controlling expenditure.
3 Administration and control.
4 Creating a climate where training can succeed.

Forecasting and Planning

In chapter 3, we discussed the importance of carrying out an analysis of training needs. This should never become a theoretical exercise which only results in paper plans and pious intentions. In many companies where there is no real appreciation by management of the economic benefits of carrying out training more systematically, it would be unprofitable to undertake a comprehensive training needs analysis, which could well take several months of valuable executive time. In this kind of situation, it is much better to spotlight areas where there is likely to be a quick payoff and start training for these skills. In practice, it is not difficult to identify those jobs line management knows instinctively require training. Admittedly there may be other, equally important, needs which are not so obvious, but the way to get systematic training accepted is by improving the present training and showing results—not by writing lengthy reports which indicate what could be done. Once results have been achieved, management will more readily accept that a training needs analysis in greater depth has practical value.

The training staff of the Perkins Manufacturing Company used this approach. The original impetus to use skills analysis training came when the training manager recognized that traditional training methods were inadequate to meet the training requirements of a new branch factory. He carried out a training needs assessment for the labour buildup for this factory and trained analysts to prepare the training courses. In fact, the new factory project was abandoned and the training manager decided to use the work done in improving training in the existing factory. He decided not to carry out a training needs analysis in this factory, but concentrated initially on training in the gear section where there was an obvious need. The results, as outlined in the last chapter, were impressive, and building on this strength the training manager was able to extend training in a planned way to other areas.

Johnson, Radley & Sons Limited are an expanding company making precision moulds for the glass industry. The managing director recognized that training had an important part to play in providing both existing skills which were in short supply, and the new skills which would be required as technology advanced. He authorized a comprehensive training needs analysis to determine the best way of meeting his demands for skill, to prepare a draft training policy for consideration by senior management, to give an indication of training staff required to meet the identified needs, and to outline a first-year plan of work for this staff with an indication of likely economic benefits which would arise from their work. The analysis showed that training needs existed for new and existing skilled and semi-skilled workers. Of equal importance for the future of the company was a regular supply of young men who would become craftsmen, draughtsmen, work study engineers, and production controllers. The company decided to meet its immediate training needs in the traditional way by training on the job. The initial systematic training effort would be a future investment. Skills analysis was used, therefore, to improve the training of apprentices, although it was recognized that once the apprentice training was under way, parts of the same training course could be used to meet the short-term training needs of skilled and semi-skilled recruits.

The managing director of Johnson, Radley Limited used a training needs analysis to point the way to improving training throughout the company. At Perkins, a much larger company, the training manager decided to improve training in one department to show what could be achieved. The comprehensive training needs analysis came later. Both men achieved their objectives—improving training on a broad front. There is thus no golden rule, other than a clear appreciation of the ultimate aim, and an understanding of the most appropriate tactics to use in a particular situation.

When the training plans have been approved by line management, it is important to ensure that adequate resources are made available to carry them out. This seems so obvious that it is unfortunate that there is often a gap between intention and ability to achieve results. What, then, constitutes 'adequate resources'? Firstly, suitable and trained training staff. It is not acknowledged sufficiently that training staff themselves require training if they are to provide an economic service. As Nancy Taylor has pointed out, 'there is a body of specialized training knowledge to be acquired and a group of skills to be developed'.[3] It is of little value seconding to training, people who are not much good at anything else.

Mr J. Mandleberg, production director of Reads Limited makes this cogent comment: 'The man to select as the analyst and the instructor is the man who can least be spared because he is the man who is best equipped to produce workers who are likely to follow his example.' This is easy to say, but Reads followed it out in practice. A systematic training scheme was prepared for setters on continuous flow can making machinery. Only one setter really understood the process and his services were in constant demand to bolster up the other setters. At considerable short-term inconvenience, this man was seconded to training. Naturally, a decision of this nature required top management backing. The results paid off. Nor was this an isolated instance in this company. Their young competent training manager suddenly died. On the day after this tragedy, the managing director, production director, and personnel manager spent several hours discussing how to replace him, considering possible names, deciding how to train the man selected, and taking short-term action to ensure training in the company continued to develop with a minimum of interruption.

This is indeed taking training seriously, recognizing it as a major activity, and providing the function with adequate staff.

The second aspect of providing adequate resources is making available proper training facilities. This does not necessarily imply expensive training centres, lavishly equipped. It does mean ensuring that trainees have machines and work on which to learn, and normally a quiet room for lectures or discussions on progress. It is unfortunate that too often old and worn out machinery is provided for trainees—machinery which experienced workers would regard as unsuitable. The standard of training facilities should match the standards normally present in production departments.

Thus, management needs to think out how its training plans are to be met. How many training staff? How much in the way of facilities? This means money and it is well to recognize that training, whether it is done well or badly, is normally expensive. The object of improving training is to cut the cost to a minimum—it will never be possible to eliminate it altogether.

Budgeting and Controlling Expenditure

The training manager, therefore, has responsibility for ensuring that the money his company allocates to training is spent wisely. He does this, as do other managers, by budgeting to ascertain the financial effects of his plans and by controlling expenditure so that as far as possible it is in line with his budget.

In practice, few companies budget for and control training expenditure well. Often, such cost control as exists is on an historical basis. At the end of the financial year, the cost of the training department is calculated and next year's expenditure assessed and taken into the company's overall budget. There are few examples of monthly cost control statements which form the basis of a dynamic control.

This is not really the training manager's fault. Accountants have paid too little attention to the costs of training. They have tended to accept 'training cost' as a necessary evil, and have failed to realize that large economies can be derived from reducing training times.

This attitude has led, too often, to a situation where the training manager has to fight for a new piece of equipment using arguments which have little relevance to the profitability of his company. The only valid basis is results, and these can be forecast and measured in financial terms.

In Great Britain, the Industrial Training Act 1964 has, undoubtedly, given an important stimulus to systematic training. The levy/grant system has brought the financial implications of training into the boardroom. Accountants now take greater notice of training cost. Yet, unfortunately, the work of training managers is still assessed too often on wrong premises. The question which should be asked is not, 'Are we maximizing our grant from a training board?' but, 'If we spend this amount on training, will we reduce our unit costs?'

A small company in the foundry industry set up elaborate procedures to identify the training which took place so that it could maximize its grant. The cost of these procedures more than outweighed the possible grant which would be recoverable from the training board. The money would have been better spent on improving the quality of some of its training.

Another, much larger company, built a new expensive training centre. This was intended to indicate that the company was taking training seriously. In practice, the quality of training did not improve—poor training now took place in an expensive building. The company would have been wiser to spend its money on improving shop-floor training procedures.

These examples indicate the importance of identifying what one ought to be doing to achieve results which lead to improvements in shop-floor performance. When these training needs have been identified, the cost of implementing improvement should be determined and cost control introduced to ensure that the performance expected is being achieved. The purpose of cost control is to enable action to be taken to bring the future in line with the plan, or to reset budgets where they have been found to be unrealistic. Any budgeting system is building for the future. Initially, training budgets may be less realistic than is desirable, but if the elements of cost have been well defined, and accurate collection of expenditure is instituted, a sound budgetary control system should be achieved in 2 to 3 years.

Although we have indicated that cost accountants in general have taken too little interest in the costs of training, this situation is now rapidly changing, at least in Great Britain, under the influence of the Industrial Training Act. Training managers are entitled to expect help from their own company's financial staff in setting up adequate cost control procedures. The two charts in Tables 9.1 and 9.2 indicate

Table 9.1. EXAMPLE OF SIMPLE CONTROL STATEMENT AGAINST PLANNED EXPENDITURE

	Month				Year to date		
	Planned expendi-ture	Actual	Variance	Cause	Planned expendi-ture	Actual	Variance
Training staff salaries							
Trainee wages							
Assistance from other departments							
Training centre⎫ Teaching aids ⎭							
Machinery and equipment							
Materials used in training							
Administration							
Utilities							
Outside services and courses							
Total							

Code for breakdown of variances by cause as for example: A = Substandard trainees; B = Labour turnover; C = Lack of materials or production work; D = Substandard machinery and equipment.

two types of control statement. The first is a simple control statement designed to give a monthly indication of actual against planned expenditure. The second, reproduced by permission of the British Association for Commercial and Industrial Education, is a more sophisticated example of one method of costing apprentice training. These are, of course, only examples. The training manager needs to work out with his company accountant a suitable method of giving adequate information which will not involve initially a complete re-organization of the company's financial reporting arrangements! The word 'initially' is used advisedly, because as experience is gained, training costs which used to be 'hidden' in overheads, are seen to be controllable and line managers will be keen to ensure that they are highlighted and kept to a minimum.

113

TABLE 9.2. ESTIMATED EXPENDITURE
for year 19   /19

Description	Craft £	Technician £	Technologist £	Graduate £	Commercial £	Total expenditure £	Description	Craft £	Technician £	Technologist £	Graduate £	Commercial £	Total expenditure £
I. Wages and salaries (taxable)							**III. Recruitment and selection:** advertising of vacancies, apprenticeship brochure, school visits, selection processes (including cost of interviewing, testing, entertainment, etc.), travelling expenses (of candidates and staff)						
(a) *Apprentices:* for time spent in works and offices and at college or courses													
(b) *Instructors:** Full time or part time (foreman or craftsman undertaking other duties)							**IV. Fees:**						
(c) *Clerical and administrative:* to include allocation of training and/or personnel department effort							(a) Fees paid to technical colleges, etc. (b) Cost of external courses and educational visits Total cost of fees						
(d) *Statutory and social:* payment for statutory and annual holidays, National Insurance, and company contribution to pension scheme							**V. Awards:** books, tools or prizes, cost of prizegiving ceremony, parents' day, etc.						
Total cost for wages and salaries							**VI. Fringe benefits:** cheap canteen meals, subsidized travel, apprentice association, sports and recreational activities, etc.						
II. Maintenance of training centre or defined training area													
(a) Rents							**VII. Accommodation:** cost of lodging allowances, provision of hostels, etc.						
(b) Rates and taxes													
(c) Depreciation of fixed assets (plant, buildings, etc.)							**VIII. Donations** and subscriptions to external bodies for training purposes						
(d) Light, fuel, and power							**IX. Any other items** please detail						
(e) Indirect labour costs (e.g. shop labourer)							GROSS COSTS						
(f) Maintenance of machine tools							CREDIT ITEMS (i.e. Value of apprentices, production if done by skilled men)						
(g) Maintenance of other equipment of a capital nature (shop tools, fixtures, furniture, equipment, and materials, etc.)							NET COSTS (i.e. Gross costs less credit items)						
(h) Consumable equipment (training material, stationery, etc.)							UNIT COSTS i.e. $\dfrac{\text{Net costs}}{\text{(Number of apprentices)}}$						
Total cost of training centre or area													

*This should include any relevant payments for overtime or bonus.
Source: A Standard Method of Costing the Training of Apprentices, obtainable from BACIE, 16 Park Crescent, Regent's Park, London, W.1.

Administration and Control

If the training department is to be well managed, the training manager needs to direct and to control the work of his staff so that they are welded into an effective unit.

This aspect of a training manager's work does not differ, of course, in principle from the responsibility of all managers to control effectively the work of others. As with other managers, the training manager needs not only to achieve results, but also to ensure that these results are in line with overall company objectives. He needs to understand, therefore, the principles of management, and the more senior he is, and the larger the organization, the more important becomes the administrative, as opposed to the technical aspects, of his work.

This is not the place to deal in detail with effective methods of administration and control. As Wilfred Brown has pointed out,[4] 'The study of administrative methods is the study of people at work, their behaviour, their relationships, the way work is split up between different roles, and the often unrecognized social institutions which companies have established and are using.' The training manager should understand these matters if he is to provide an effective service to other managers.

Specifically, he needs to plan the work of his staff, ensure that they understand their objectives and the results expected, and to check on their performance. He needs to plan ahead to ensure that facilities are available. For example, the typing load in the preparation of manuals must be foreseen or work will be held up.

When Perkins first introduced skills analysis training, the training manager had a staff of ten analysts. Between them they produced thirty training manuals in 6 months. This speed of output was made possible because the training manager programmed the work of each analyst, ensured that there was no duplication of effort, and held regular co-ordinating meetings with his team.

Creating a Climate where Training can Succeed

Although the ultimate responsibility for effective training is line management's, the training officer can do much to ensure the success of their efforts. He needs to discuss training with managers, foremen, and shop stewards on a continuing basis. His is no chairborne job—success lies in getting out and about, discussing training with others in their work situation, rather than in the isolation of his own office. Only in this way is he likely to succeed in convincing others that his training recommendations are relevant to their needs. If he observes training problems in the work situation, he will be better equipped to lead others to formulate their training needs—to isolate problems of learning which are truly training problems, from areas of difficulty which should be solved in some other way.

In a light engineering company, management planned to expand production rapidly. Training staff were asked to introduce skills analysis training and facilities and trainees were made available. Fortunately, the training officer was also a good manager and he foresaw that the results of reducing traditional training times by two thirds on the main assembly line, where training was to start, would create bottlenecks in production in the sub-assembly sections. Anticipated production schedules were revised, and training plans modified, to ensure that the build-up in production was steady throughout the production unit.

Of course, this example does not imply that line managers cannot foresee the results of changes in training procedure. It does mean, however, that the training manager, because he knows how good training can increase output, is in a position to draw the attention of other managers to the implications of his efforts. It demonstrates clearly that he understands, and can convince others of his understanding, that training is not an end in itself, but only a means to achieve production at a lower cost. The training manager who concentrates on what he can contribute, who goes out and sees the problems for himself, is the man who will do most to create a situation where 'training' will succeed.

If senior management appoints the right man and gives him the opportunity to contribute, the job of a training officer is full of interest. As Nancy Taylor has said,[5] 'The careful selection and training of an appropriate individual who has the energy, expertise, and enthusiasm to head up the training function is the cornerstone on which a company should build a sound and effective training programme.' The job, if it is to be performed successfully, requires that the man, who has to deal with day-to-day training problems, works in close association with line managers so that he fulfils their actual needs, and yet is accorded sufficient time for the chairborne activity to plan and control the work of his staff, and to co-ordinate the total effort of the training department. Here, indeed, is a fine mixture of management activity. We must now discuss to whom he should report, and the total organization and use of the training function within a company.

References

1 *The Effective Executive:* P. F. Drucker, Heinemann, 1967.
2 'Automation and Skill': E. R. F. W. Crossman. *Problems of Progress in Industry*, No. 9, D.S.I.R.
3 *Selecting and Training the Training Officer:* A. L. T. Taylor. Institute of Personnel Management, 1966.
4 *Exploration in Management:* W. Brown. Heinemann, 1960.
5 *Selecting and Training the Training Officer:* A. L. T. Taylor. Institute of Personnel Management, 1966.

10. The organization of training

The chart in Fig. 8.1 (chapter 8) indicates the various functions within a company which have an influence on the successful introduction of systematic non-supervisory training in an organization. In the chart, the place of training staff was by design left vague. Their place will vary to meet the needs of the local situation, and will depend on the current organization of a company, its past attitude to training, the abilities and personalities of the people involved, and the general background of industrial relations.

In this chapter, we examine these matters in more detail, because as training needs, and the importance of the training function, become more specifically recognized, so the training function expands and its place in the organization requires to be thought out carefully. As David King has pointed out,[1] 'The authority and responsibility for the training function will need to be reviewed and clarified throughout the organization.'

We have stressed previously the point that training is a line management responsibility, and that the role of training specialists is to advise, help, clarify needs, prepare training schemes, and often take major responsibility for running them, always remembering, of course, that if they do this they are, as it were, acting *in loco parentis*.

Instructors and Analysts

Before considering to whom the training manager should report, we may find it easier to discuss the place of the training instructor in the organization. Normally, one of two procedures presents itself: either he reports to the training manager or to the departmental head, normally the supervisor, on whose behalf he undertakes the training.

In our experience, either solution can work well, and often the decision will depend on where the actual training takes place. For example, at Wedgwood's, training is given in each production department. The instructors report to the departmental supervisor, while the training officer is responsible for ensuring that the training is of a high standard. The reader may well ask 'what happens if there is a serious conflict of opinion between the supervisor and the training officer?' The short answer is that the supervisor would prevail. However, this should be an academic question (and it is at Wedgwood's) where the importance of training is well recognized throughout the company, and the training officer is well aware that the training given must meet line management's requirements. In fact, it is true to say that in general where there are serious clashes of opinion between training staff and supervisors, the root cause is that the training scheme is not appropriate to that particular situation.

In companies where it has been decided that training will take place in a separate training centre, remote from the shop floor, it is usually more convenient for the instructor to report to the training manager. The only word of warning which needs to be uttered, in these situations, is that extra care must be taken to ensure that the training given matches line management's changing needs.

In larger companies, where the training manager has a team of skills analysts to assist him, they will normally report to him, though there are cases where analysts report to divisional line management, either permanently or on secondment.

The Training Manager

This brings us to the central, and much discussed, question, to whom does the training manager report? A great deal of 'emotion' is normally generated in 'training circles' whenever this question is debated. The energy used could possibly be better utilized in improving training rather than in discussing who one's boss should be. The answer depends, of course, on local factors, and we shall give some examples which indicate that training can be successful in a variety of organizational situations. This is hardly surprising—what does cause comment is that training officers so often get heated when discussing the matter.

In purely theoretical terms, it is our opinion that training is part of the function in industry which has to do with people. This function is normally called 'personnel management', and as personnel departments increasingly lose their 'welfare' image and develop a managerial and cost conscious outlook, so we will no doubt find that the training manager will report to the personnel director. In the meantime, there are often good and sufficient local reasons why he should report to someone else.

The size of the company is also of great importance. The executive responsible for training in a medium-sized company may be responsible for managerial as well as non-supervisory training. In a small company, this may be only a part-time job; in some medium-sized companies, he is also the personnel manager. In large companies, the training officer responsible for skills analysis training may report to a more senior training manager. There are endless permutations. What is important is to ensure that the man is not debarred from doing an effective job because of some organizational defect. In some companies, his pay or 'status' may be so low that the line managers with whom he works feel, probably correctly, that senior management regard training as of low importance. It is, therefore, more important to select the right man, pay him properly, and have him report to an executive who carries 'weight' within the organization.

The following are some examples of where training can be placed in the organization. The only thing which the companies have in common is that skills analysis training is highly successful, well integrated with line management's needs, and saving the companies a great deal of money in training cost.

Company A

This is a company employing 1,000 people with an established personnel function. The training officer reports to the production director, and is separated organizationally from the personnel department. His staff consists of a typist, one analyst, and training instructors who report to him.

Company B

This is a company employing 250 people with no established personnel manager. The 'training officer' is responsible only for apprentice and operator training, though it is envisaged that in due course he will become responsible for management training. He reports to the production director, and is responsible for selection and engagement of trainees.

Company C

A large company employing 6,000 people, where the training staff are part of the personnel function. The executive responsible for skills analysis training reports to a more senior training manager, who in turn reports to the personnel director.

Company D

A company employing 1,250 people, where the training officer reports to the industrial engineer, who in turn reports to the production director.

Company E

A company employing 400 people, where the executive responsible for skills analysis training is also the chief work study engineer. He carries out his own skills analysis, and prepares training courses, but also supervises the work of three work study men.

Company F

A very small company of thirteen people in a highly specialized trade which employed a consultant to carry out the skills analysis. The chief, and then only, executive, ensured that new learners were taught using the training manual produced by the consultant.

Company G

A company of 7,600 people, where all training had long been an established part of the personnel function. Initially, systematic operator training was established as part of personnel, but now, when it is firmly entrenched, the operator training officer reports to the works manager.

All of which goes to show that it is more important to take the decision to train effectively, than it is to worry unduly as to where the person responsible for the function should be located on the organization chart. In a company which is proposing to introduce skills analysis training and set up a training function, the line manager who takes the decision will, in any event, have to spare time to ensure that the new approach is successful. We shall be covering this aspect in more detail in the next chapter.

Product Planning and Training

So far, we have discussed the formal organization of training within a company. The remainder of this chapter deals with the importance of using the training function effectively, wherever it may be formally located on the organization chart.

In a period of great technical change, we have stressed already the need to forecast training requirements. In simple terms, this means determining the role people will play in the new technology, assessing their training needs, and taking steps to meet them. Take, for example, the case of the company which decides to introduce more highly mechanized machinery to replace individual machines producing the same product. At first sight, this is purely a technical problem. Instead of a number of individual machine tools, the decision is made to link them together in an automatic flow line. Fewer people will be employed, the rate of production will increase, and costs will come down. The following is a typical case of what can happen.

A company installed a £3 million mechanized transfer line. The machining operations were almost identical with those carried out previously on a number of individual semi-automatic machines. The major difference was that in future the product would be 'automatically' transferred from one machine to the next, thus speeding up production and reducing cost. Two years after the new line was installed, excessive downtime was still being experienced. Lost production had to be made up in overtime, and other excess costs were incurred. What had gone wrong? The official explanation was teething troubles, but more than this was involved. One major factor was that the company had not thought through the training needs of people involved in this type of machinery—they had assumed that experienced workers used to the old technology would be able to handle the new. The engineers were simplifying work; the tasks of workers would be easier, not more difficult, to perform. A period of familiarization, not basic training, would be all that was required.

Unfortunately, this is a common fallacy. Management too often fails to recognize that in a man/machine system of great complexity the role of people in closing the 'loop' is vital. No complex machine system will work completely unaided. People are needed to maintain it, take action when it breaks down, and most importantly to anticipate serious trouble before it arises. S. D. M. King has already stressed the importance of thinking through the way work roles are assigned in this type of technology. As he says,[2] 'No sweeping generalizations can be made. Each job must be studied in detail to find out what decisions have been assigned to the operator.' Maintenance staff require to be trained in diagnostic skills, so that faults can be traced rapidly and the machine restarted. Above all, training is needed to improve the flow of information between the operator and the maintenance mechanic, so that breakdown time is minimized.

The training officer obviously has a part to play in all this. All too often, however, he is called in too late, after the machinery has been installed and trouble is being encountered. A surer solution is for management to invest him with the responsibility, at the planning stage, for assisting the project team in determining the role of people in the system. In this way, the importance of human beings in the man/machine system will be constantly recognized, the training officer will be able to prepare draft courses of instruction at an early stage, and such training will be highly relevant to individual needs. Above all, everyone concerned with the new installation will be constantly reminded that a machine or process is, in the end, only as good as the people who look after it.

It may be objected that engineers are capable of thinking in these terms, unaided by a training specialist. No doubt this is true, but it is equally true that in practice they seem to pay more attention to 'things' than 'people'. To redress the balance there is a sound case for introducing, at an early stage, a specialist who is himself trained to think in terms of work. That is the nature and content of the tasks which must be performed to make the system viable. The skills analyst is trained in these matters and has a valuable contribution to make.

Day-to-Day Problems

Many problems connected with training arise on a day-to-day basis, especially where specialized training has been recently introduced. Here are some examples which show that even when the formal organization of the training function has been worked out, difficulties will still arise. Although each case is unique, in the sense that the same situation is unlikely to occur elsewhere, they have one thing in common—the need for management to ensure that the results of the training are properly used.

A large company set up a training school for riveters. Initially, it was run on T.W.I. lines, trainees being passed to the production departments capable of performing the job at the correct quality. The buildup of piecework speed was left to the trainees themselves when they arrived on the production line. In practice, this meant that they worked with experienced riveters for a period acting largely as 'assistants'. Skills analysis training was introduced, and the training section started to send riveters to the production department capable of working at an experienced worker's standard of speed and quality. Furthermore, this standard was achieved in exactly the same length of training time as under the T.W.I. system. The production foremen experienced some difficulty in altering patterns of work in the department to cope with these new riveters. Previously, they had performed 'odd jobs' while assisting other riveters. Now, they were capable of doing an experienced man's work and the foremen were faced with the problem of who was to perform the 'odd jobs'. Clearly, the answer lay in some alteration of duties and this in fact took place.

In another company, trainees were traditionally given simple work to perform. The training period was measured in years rather than months, and learners in their first year managed to produce enough work to meet the company's output needs for this simple-to-make product. The introduction of skills analysis training radically altered the situation. The simple work was still given to trainees, but more complex work had to be fed in quickly when it was discovered that the first group of trainees had produced a year's supply of the simple-to-make product within the first month.

These two examples indicate the need to train supervisors to use the greater skills of trainees. It takes time to change attitudes and well-established practices. In another company, new starters were trained to be versatile over a range of operations, but little benefit was derived until supervision had been persuaded to abandon their long-standing practice of only using new starters on one operation for several months.

Another common problem relates to trainees being placed in work for which they have not been trained.

124

Skills analysis training was introduced in a textile machining factory. Unfortunately, during the analysis period it was not recognized that although the skills required by the machinist appeared to be the same throughout the year, differences in weight and texture of material were of great significance. When the work was analysed, only one type of cloth was being worked on—by the time the trainees had completed their training, another type of cloth was being used. Not surprisingly, the learners failed to achieve the results expected and the future courses had to be drastically remodelled before success was achieved.

This is an excellent example indicating that a training course is only as good as the analysis on which it is based. It is also an example of inadequate analysis of training need, which is a pitfall often encountered in training circles.

Training officers often complain that trainees are transferred to production departments before training is complete in order to help meet a production crisis, on the assumption that any production is better than none. This situation normally arises where trainees are being taught a variety of skills on varying products. As it is axiomatic that a person being taught systematically will produce more than one left to fend for himself, the answer lies in a rapid modification of the training course to help production meet their needs. There is no reason why training should not be interrupted in this way, provided that the learner is still receiving detailed instruction. When the immediate crisis is over, the remainder of the training can be given in the normal way. Production work should, however, be fed into the training section to ensure that the learners continue to be taught to achieve experienced worker's standard on the work which is needed urgently.

The use of a training centre in this way can be of great value. Short production runs which have to be fitted into a normal production schedule are often the bane of a supervisor's life. Training centres, however, should be eager to produce these short runs. The programme of training can be adapted to use them to give a variety of practice. Too often, it is assumed that learners will not produce saleable work. The whole object of skills analysis training is that trainees will produce large quantities of it during the training period.

The Effective Training of Small Numbers of Trainees

Skills analysis is an expensive undertaking in terms of the time required to analyse completely a complex task. There are many instances where a company, with, say, a low labour turnover, requires to train only one or two men a year for a particular job. Suppose the real training time to an experienced worker's standard is 4 months, and that using a full application of skills analysis, the equivalent training time could be reduced to between 6 and 8 weeks. In most cases, it is extremely doubtful whether the investment would be justified in terms of time and money. After all people *can* learn 'sitting by Nellie'; they have done so for decades and the theme of this book is that improved training must show results in terms of money. Do we then give up and say that where only a few trainees are required each year, the most economic way of training is the traditional method? The answer is likely to be 'no'. In all jobs of the type we are discussing, there are certain aspects of knowledge or of physical skill which are crucial and usually the most difficult to learn. These are the areas which can be isolated and analysed relatively cheaply. Once the learning difficulties have been understood, someone in the department, often a foreman trained in T.W.I., can devote the time required to pass on the results of the analysis to the new starter in a systematic manner. Thus, steps will have been taken to train in a positive way the important and difficult areas of the task—the rest can be picked up 'on the job'. The total training time, using this aproach, may be reduced only slightly, but the cost of the limited analysis will be repaid in terms of fewer costly learning mistakes and the likelihood of the learner becoming a useful member of the department more rapidly, because he knows that someone is taking the trouble to teach him his job.

A company employed a number of men in a radial drilling operation. The numbers requiring training did not justify a full skills analysis, but the training officer was asked to help because of certain quality problems. In two days, he was able to identify the areas of knowledge which caused learning difficulty. From this analysis, he prepared a simple on the job training scheme which taught only this part of the job. No analysis of physical skills was undertaken. Total learning time to acquire speed skills was not reduced, but the company saved over £1,000 per year in reduction of rectification cost.

Even though only small numbers of trainees may be required each year, the cost of a full skills analysis may be repaid by using it to retrain existing operators to a higher level. In other cases, a full skills analysis may be the only way of perceiving skills possessed only by one or two individuals who have been with the company many years. It is surprising how often companies leave themselves at risk in this way. The people concerned are usually so reliable, both in their work and attendance, that it is apparently forgotten that they may one day retire, become sick, or suddenly leave from some other cause. Analysing their skills at least ensures that a replacement can be trained rapidly if the need arises.

Another common problem of small numbers is found on assembly lines, where each work position appears to be different. However, analysis will indicate that there are certain common areas of skill used in each work position. Table 10.1 indicates the way in which such an analysis is undertaken. The ticks show the skills required in each work position, and it is then possible to devise off the job training exercises which will teach the common skills used. In the example given, clearly the use of a plain screwdriver, hammer, and so on needs to be taught. The use of a combination screwdriver would be left to be picked up on the job. By using this approach, new starters can be given coaching and practice off the job in a major portion of the skills required, while detailed training is given by traditional methods on the job. The example used is from light assembly work, where training time was reduced from 12 to 6 weeks with a marked improvement in quality.

Table 10. 1

TYPE OF TOOL	WORK POSITION								
	1	2	3	4	5	6	7	8	9
Plain screwdriver	√	√	√	√	√	√		√	√
Box spanner	√	√	√	√	√	√		√	√
Spring screwdriver	√	√			√				
Combination screwdriver				√					
Pump screwdriver	√				√				
Spanner	√				√				
Hammer	√		√	√		√	√	√	
Bender and three prong pliers	√		√						
Air tools			√			√		√	
Feeler gauges with special 'feel'		√		√					√
Pliers			√			√	√	√	
Applicator			√					√	√
Spring hook and tweezers						√	√		
Special tooling and gauging, etc.	√	√		√				√	√

In engineering companies using a variety of machine tools, the number of new starters on any one type of machine is often limited. Investigations have shown that even time-served craftsmen often require a considerable learning period before they can achieve an experienced worker's standard, particularly when the class of work is outside their previous experience. Many of the companies concerned have established apprentice training schools, and after the first year of basic training the boys are given 'training' on each type of machine. Clearly, the numbers requiring training on any one machine in a year include both apprentices and new starters from outside. If the apprentice training is largely slanted to a company's own needs (as it should be), then there is likely to be a strong case for setting up skills analysis based training for each type of work. The same course will serve for apprentices and outside entrants, though, of course, the latter will only be taught the part of the total course which deals with the machines on which they are expected to work.

Johnson Radley Limited use this approach. After the first year basic training, the apprentices are given a short skills analysis based course on one of the types of machine used in production, for example, engraving. They are then expected to work on this machine for a few weeks before moving on to the next part of their training. Outside entrants are also engaged, and those who are engaged to work on the engraving machines are given exactly the same course as the apprentices to ensure that they can meet the company's high performance standards of quality.

Dealing with the Training Crisis

Many companies find a sudden need to expand production in one department, possibly for a temporary period, to meet the requirements of a special order. Skills analysis training can be of great value in these situations, even though the necessary analysis work may be on a once only basis. There are too many instances in our experience of companies, when faced with this problem, seeking to overcome it by engaging labour in excess of requirements, and suffering from a high labour turnover and large excess costs as a result.

A large international company with a plant in North America found itself faced with a situation where they could capture an extra 10 per cent of the market if production was expanded rapidly to meet demand. This attractive prospect led to a minor crisis in the production department concerned in which handwork of a very high quality standard was required. Work study standards established a labour force requirement of 130. All 'training' was of the exposure variety, with no instructors or training syllabi. New starters were placed with the existing trained operators and left to fend for themselves. The large-scale production demand lasted for one year. In this period the department engaged 630 operators, of whom 580 or 93 per cent left within the first 12 months. Rectification costs were enormous, and a very conservative estimate of total cost incurred was £100,000. It is stated that the market requirement was met—but at what a cost!

A better and simpler solution would have been to analyse the skills involved and train the new operators before placing them on production. An estimate of the total training time which would have been required was 6–8 weeks. Undoubtedly, if this had been done, labour turnover would have been cut and rectification costs much reduced. The cost of the analysis and setting up the training section on the shop floor would have been of the order of £1,000. Two full-time instructors would have been required, costing say, £4,000. (North American salaries.) Against this, a reduction of 50 per cent in scrap alone could have been expected, saving £50,000. Reduction of labour turnover by at least 50 per cent would have saved another £20,000. ($48,000)

An engineering company captured a large order involving the assembly of large metal components. Various processes were involved, but much of the work comprised welding. The estimated labour intake requirement was forty people, most of whom would require training in the welding techniques involved. The company looked at the problem as a total project. Methods, jigging, and fixtures had to be worked out, a suitable wages policy agreed with the unions concerned, and plans laid down for training. Although we are only concerned here with the training aspect, it is important to stress that the efforts of the training officer were closely integrated at every stage with the other members of the planning team. A special temporary welding school was established in part of the production department and training given in welding in various awkward positions before the parts arrived for main assembly. The labour intake was carefully phased so that by the time production began a labour force, largely trained to deal with it, was already assembled. The results of the total exercise were impressive. Production and cost targets were met and labour turnover can be considered minimal, where a large intake of labour was required in an area where the labour pool is small.

The difference in the approach in these examples is marked. In the first, labour is treated as so many 'hands' to produce the management's requirements as best they may. In the second, management recognized that success lay in recruiting, training, and motivating a new labour force prior to actual production need. Training had a part to play in all this—but success lay in the integrated approach.

The Training Function Which Dies on its Feet

In a chapter which deals with the organization of training, it is perhaps appropriate to mention the problem of those companies which have a long-established training function, where training has 'ossified'. The leaders of yesterday, if not exactly the laggards of today, are at best no more than halfway up the league. We think there are in the main three causes of this situation. First, the training staff have failed to implement new advances in training techniques. Skills analysis today, for example, is a vastly more versatile animal than when the Seymour brothers first developed it. How many apprentice training schools, for example, have used this approach to first year training? Secondly, training staff have failed to review and modify their schemes to meet changing line management need. There are, unfortunately, examples of training centres imparting redundant skills to trainees and failing to revise syllabi. Thirdly, training staff have become complacent and fail to review their work on a cost effective basis. A thorough periodical audit of a training function is a necessary discipline.

All of which brings us back to the need for management to ensure that the training function meets its operational needs. It matters little to whom training staff report, provided that they are dynamic, of real value to line management, and pay for their keep. In the next chapter, we discuss the steps line management should take to ensure that an effective non-supervisory training function is established in their company.

References

1 *Training Within the Organization:* D. King. Tavistock Publications, 1964.
2 *Vocational Training in View of Technological Change:* S. D. M. King, Organisation for Economic co-operation, 1960 (E.P.A. Project No. 418).

Part IV

11. Guide lines for management action

This chapter is concerned with the ways in which line managers can translate the subject matter of this book into effective action. Obviously, senior management must make an initial decision as to whether it wishes to set up an effective non-supervisory training function at all. But commitment to a principle is not enough. Both the philosophy behind training and the provision of effective means to secure it must be there.

A company engaged in precision engineering had a problem in recruiting and training sufficient staff for its expanding business. In one department, training time was measured in years rather than in months. The potential cost savings available from better training were clear to local management. Consultants were asked to survey the problem, and submitted their report. This confirmed that there was a training need, but stressed the complex nature of the analysis which would have to be undertaken. Nothing happened for a year and then the company appointed a training officer. Another year went by and the training officer, recognizing the need for more specialist assistance, asked for help. Again the consultants submitted proposals and again nothing happened. Three years after the initial recognition of need, the position is substantially the same as it was at the beginning. At a minimum estimate, £50,000 has been wasted by the equivocation and the reluctance of senior management to commit themselves to the provision of the necessary resources for setting up an effective training function.

The major lesson to be learned from this sad case is that it is not enough to appoint a training officer and expect him to provide answers to what is essentially a management problem. In one sense, managers exist because they as individuals are charged with more responsibility for results than they can personally achieve. So they have to employ people as subordinates to help them. It is a sound basic principle that if one employs someone to do what one wants, fairly explicit instructions should be given not only as to what is expected, but how to achieve it, if the subordinate is unable to produce satisfactory results. Thus, managers cannot abdicate from their ultimate responsibility for training—indeed the more closely they take an interest in it, the more likely they are to achieve, through their subordinates, the results which are expected of them by their own superior managers. Training specialists can help and guide—they can never supplant the manager in his responsibility for providing adequate training.

What, then, should a manager do to decide whether his own non-supervisory training arrangements are adequate to meet his needs? As a manager, he will recognize that training, in any form, is expensive and also that cost is being incurred in one way or another until an experienced worker's standard has been reached.

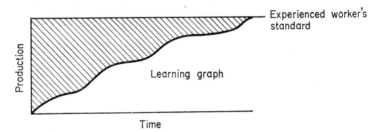

Fig. 11.1 A representation of the loss of production by trainees not yet to experienced worker's standard

In Fig. 11.1, all the area to the left of the learning graph represents loss of production and therefore loss of money, even if individuals are covering their basic rate by piecework earnings before they attain experienced worker's standard.

Improving training must be cost effective. The extra cost of improving the training must be less than the anticipated savings from increased production, reduction in scrap, or rectification cost and so on. So a manager, before deciding whether training specialists are needed at all, would be wise to organize his own brief training needs analysis in cost terms. We covered this aspect in chapter 3: here are a few reminders of some key indices to examine.

136

First, look at the real length of learning time to achieve experienced worker's standard. Make a cost estimate of the loss of production, and multiply this figure by the number of people who have to be trained each year.

Second, look at the labour turnover figures of those who leave during the training period. Make a rough calculation of how much money is spent each year in direct wages and overheads for no production. For example, if a job takes 12 weeks to achieve experienced worker's standard, the following table of wages, Table 11.1, for no production is typical. In a large department with high turnover, this figure can be quite substantial, and it takes no account of value of lost production or scrap.

Table 11. 1

Week	Percentage Production of an Experienced Worker	Percentage Time Paid for no Production	Cost, if Direct Wage + Overhead is £20 Per Week
1	20	80	£16
2	30	70	£14
3	40	60	£12
4	40	60	£12
5	45	55	£11
6	50	50	£10
7	60	40	£ 8
8	70	30	£ 6
9	80	20	£ 4
10	85	15	£ 3
11	90	10	£ 2
12	95	5	£ 1
TOTAL DIRECT WAGE LOSS FOR EACH TRAINEE			£99 ($240)

Third, examine scrap or rectification costs of learners' work throughout the training period. In some companies, the figure can be startlingly high.

Fourth, where there are machines, examine the downtime figures. Carry out the calculation like this:

1 Calculate the anticipated production if all the machines worked 100 per cent of the normal working week.
2 Subtract planned time for changeovers and planned maintenance —but nothing else.
3 Examine records to show actual production achieved, and express this as a percentage of (1) minus (2).

If the resulting figure is less than 90 per cent, it is worthwhile trying to find out the causes. All the reasons won't be training failures—but many of them will be.

These four indices are rough guides, but they should be sufficient for any manager to decide whether he has a training problem large enough to do something about. So having decided to take action, who should be charged with the responsibility? Here there can be no firm guide lines other than the need to ensure that a training specialist is available to give help and advice. Some companies appoint a full-time training manager to advise and help line management; in others, a part-time responsibility is all that is required. Whoever is appointed, it should be remembered that training people need training themselves. Don't expect this to happen on a one week course. Training is a major activity and there is a lot to learn, as we saw in chapter 7.

Having chosen, and appointed, a suitable individual, work out with him training objectives and standards of performance. Make these as precise as possible, based possibly on the rough training needs assessment outlined earlier in this chapter. Remember, also, that the analysis on which sound training is based takes time, especially when one is new to the task. So don't expect training schemes to spring up overnight. If they do, they are unlikely to be soundly based. It is much better for the first job to be really effective, because then other managers and supervisors will see the value of systematic training. So choosing the first pilot area is important. Here are some points to consider:

Current training time to experienced worker's standard should be over 6 weeks and preferably under 18 months. The cost effective calculation should show clearly that a marked improvement in training time will bring financial benefits.

The supervisor should recognize that a training problem exists, although he may be sceptical as to whether it can be ameliorated.

Having agreed in the first place to train, give the training specialist time and facilities to do a good job, and then review the results achieved. At this stage, the full financial benefits can only be assessed on trends. That is that the reduced training times, if maintained, can be shown to lead to reduction in training cost. More important for the manager having to make a decision whether to extend this form of training or not is the reaction of middle and junior management. Do the trainees meet their requirements? Do they feel that the training staff have helped them? Even though the new method of training has involved changes in procedures, are they willing to integrate these new ideas into the day-to-day running of their department? If the

138

reactions are favourable, it is a safe bet that the training officer has made an effective contribution and that other departmental heads will be interested in revising their training arrangements. A manager must also recognize that in some cases the long-term benefits of training may well outweigh the short-term payoff. So a decision will now have to be made as to where the training staff should operate next. Circumstances vary, but this may well be the stage when a more comprehensive training needs assessment, as outlined in chapter 3, could usefully be undertaken. We have referred to training committees in chapter 8, and in some companies it is useful to discuss the results of the training needs assessment with senior departmental managers sitting as a training committee. This has the advantage of highlighting immediate needs and priorities. It is important not to overload the training staff, or to expect quick results by reducing the time taken to analyse the job for which training is to be given. Analysis is a form of capital investment and penny pinching will not give adequate results. This does not, of course, mean that the amount of analysis should be out of proportion to the results expected, but rather that sufficient time must always be allowed to enable a satisfactory answer to be given to the question, 'What exactly does a new starter need to know to perform this job competently?' The great danger is expecting too much, too soon, from inadequate resources. The training committee could well discuss ways of enabling the training staff to be augmented on a temporary basis to meet immediate priorities.

In one company, the training committee had agreed a forward programme for the training department for the next 6 months. This was ambitious but attainable, if diversionary activities were kept to a minimum. After 2 months, a training need of some urgency arose in a department which was not included in the programme. Rather than change the agreed programme of analysis, the training officer suggested that the department head of the section asking for help should second two of his best men for 6 months to work as analysts. The training officer trained them in analytical techniques and supervised their work. Not only was the problem overcome, but the two men seconded gained useful knowledge and understanding of their own department's work during their period as analysts. Working as a training analyst is a useful means of developing people.

Managers, supervisors, and training staff should all recognize that the purpose of non-supervisory training is to help people to learn new skills fast. This applies as much to internal transfers within a company as it does to starters coming in from outside. Training proposals must, therefore, be realistic in terms of what has to be learnt, rather than theoretical in concentrating on the marginal. This is particularly important when dealing with new and complex machinery or processes.

In some cases, we have seen long training schemes which cover all aspects of a process down to the last detail. It is clear that much of the syllabus was worked out in an office answering the question 'What is it desirable for a person to know if he is to work competently in this plant?' Unfortunately, this is the wrong question asked in the wrong place. A much better result would have been achieved by going on the shop floor, observing what people were expected to do, understanding the causes of failure, and drawing up a preliminary syllabus of training, answering the question, 'To enable an individual to perform the duties allocated to him, what exactly does he have to know?' We have used the words 'preliminary syllabus of training', as the answers to the question may well spotlight a need to rethink the way in which the process is manned and the duties of each individual. The results of this exercise would, of course, alter the training syllabus.

It is obvious that the analysis of knowledge and skill required will reveal information which is not of a strictly training nature. One of the major benefits of training staff working closely with line management is that this information can be used as a basis for management action. This is not to say that management is unaware of the problems, rather that the importance of solving them is put in a new perspective.

At Read's Limited, for example, management was well aware that the machinery needed overhaul and that preventive maintenance procedures should be instituted. The training analysis for the mechanics looking after the can-making machinery strongly underlined this. It became evident that no training was likely to bring significant benefits unless certain machinery overhauls and better preventive maintenance were undertaken. Management took the necessary action at the same time that the training course was developed, and the result was highly successful, though it was evident that neither the maintenance nor the training could separately have conferred the same benefit.

In another company starting production on a new product, the training analysis showed that people on the final assembly line were failing to produce at the quality and speed expected because there were major problems involved with some of the sub-assemblies from a previous department. An additional problem arose from the forecast production after retraining, in that if targets were achieved, the supply of sub-assemblies would be inadequate. An urgent need was revealed, therefore, for retraining in the sub-assembly department to enable both quality and output to be improved. This in turn led to a complete review of production targets, which had been set at an unrealistically high level, and the planned build up of production was revised to achieve the possible rather than the desirable.

Both these examples show how necessary it is for training staff and line management to work closely together as a team. Some senior managers have taken steps to ensure a close relationship by charging the services of training staff to the departments using them. This, at least, ensures that line management is encouraged to get value for its money.

One production director has a useful approach to the problem. He informed his department managers that the services of training staff were available to them. He stressed that none of them need feel any obligation to use this central service if they felt able to deal with their training requirements unaided. However, he also pointed out that he would feel unable to accept the reason of inadequate operators as an excuse for failure to meet production or quality targets. This provided a strong incentive for department managers to use the services of the training specialist!

Each senior manager will have his own approach to setting the optimum conditions whereby training staff can be integrated into the day-to-day life of his company. The method used is less important than ensuring that this result is achieved, for this is the only way in which training becomes an effective management function rather than a desirable ancillary activity.

The Manager and His Training Officer

If senior managers expect their training officers to act as managers, they should be prepared to treat them as such. In our experience, there are far too many instances of training staff being the last to hear of new developments.

A company received a large order for a new product. It was clear that not only would new methods of production be required, but that staff would have to be recruited and trained. A great deal of preparation work was done by production management, work study, and planning staff. One week before production was scheduled to begin, the personnel department was asked to supply seventy extra people. This was bad enough, as no proper selection procedures could be devised in the short time available. What was worse was the fact that it was clear that most of the new recruits would require training if production schedules were to be met. With the best will in the world the training officer could not have prepared and mounted a training course for this operation in a week. To his credit he tried—it was not surprising that he failed and the build up of production was slower than anticipated.

The failure here was clearly that of line management. It was yet another instance of the false assumption that most people will learn most things rapidly if they come under the general title 'semi-skilled'. It is high time all managements recognized that there is a great deal to learn in most so called 'semi-skilled' jobs, if the person is to produce at the expected speed and quality.

Let us now consider what training staff have to do to prepare and run a training course which is intended to achieve satisfactory results. Managers should read this list not only to understand how much work is entailed, but also to be able to check that it has been done.

1 *Establish a Syllabus of Training*
What skills and knowledge have to be acquired? Are all new starters expected to be able to deal with, at the initial stage, every product which goes through the department? This is unlikely, as often 80 per cent of production is concerned with 25 per cent of the products, and the remaining 20 per cent of production, covering 75 per cent of the products, is given to the most experienced employees. However, the supervisory staff must make up its mind, and the training officer will expect help from the supervisor in establishing the syllabus.

2 *Establish Reference Data*
How long does it take to achieve the standards expected? This may well have been elicited at the training needs analysis stage, but the

142

information is important if a valid 'before' and 'after' comparison is to be made for control purposes.

3 *Inform Workers of the 'New' Approach to Training*
The analysis of physical skills and knowledge must be carried out on the shop floor. Therefore, employee goodwill is essential. A greater degree of co-operation is required than for, say, a work study investigation, as much of the information required cannot be seen, but is in the employee's head. The analyst needs to know 'how' success is achieved, not just 'what' is done, and only the worker on the job can tell him. Supervisors can do a great deal to help training staff receive the help they need.

4 *Analyse Knowledge and Skills*
Chapters 4 and 5 indicate how much is involved here. Sufficient analysis must take place to ensure that a learner can be given positive instruction in 'how to perform' at all the major stages of the learning process.

5 *Establish a Standard Method for Training Purposes*
Usually, the analysis will show that experienced workers use varying methods in achieving satisfactory results. These methods vary from worker to worker and often one detailed method is as good as another, but to avoid confusion in a learner's mind one standard method should be established for training purposes. Training staff need to discuss this with the supervisors who should have the final decision. A word of warning here. Sometimes the analyst will be able to discover improved methods which can be discussed with supervisors and the work study department, if they are clearly of great significance. Small or minor improvements can be ignored, as it is undesirable to initiate too many changes which cannot be seen to be obviously desirable by the working group, whose co-operation is needed for training purposes.

6 *Check Analysis*
When completed, the analysis must be checked for accuracy. There are various ways of doing this. The best is for the analyst to perform the operation working from his own analysis. He will soon discover any points which have been insufficiently analysed. In some operations, this is not possible, and a check can be made by observing other workers and anticipating what they will be doing next as the work proceeds. An unexplained movement or action discloses an area where further analysis may be required. A third method is to observe

learners on the operation. The analyst should be able to spot immediately what they are doing wrongly and how they can correct the mistake.

7 *Prepare Preliminary Exercises*
The analysis must now be examined to enable it to be broken down into logical teaching units. This may involve the preparation of special preliminary exercises to give practice in the special skills required. Target times for each teaching unit must be established.

8 *Prepare an Overall Timetable*
The next step is to prepare an overall timetable for the course on the lines discussed in chapter 6.

9 *Prepare a Faults Museum*
It is important to formalize the quality specification for the stage of the process for which training is being given. Additionally, the analysis of faults must be undertaken and a faults museum be assembled for training purposes.

10 *Select and Train Instructors*
The selection and training of instructors was discussed in chapter 7. This is clearly a vital step and a hurried decision should not be made. A reminder: above all, do not pressurize the training officer into accepting someone unsuitable just because management cannot think of anything else for the individual concerned to do. Remember that the proper person may well be the one who, apparently, can least be spared. Further, when the instructor has been selected, ensure he receives adequate training.

11 *Decide where Training will Take Place*
We discussed the pros and cons of having a training centre, away from the production department, in chapter 6. Expense obviously enters into the calculation, but it is more important to ensure that if the training is given away from the production department, that supervisors continue to take a personal interest in the training being given.

12 *Select Trainees*
The selection of trainees was discussed in chapter 7. It is no use attempting to train people who do not possess the basic aptitudes to profit from their training. Training schemes have been known to fail because management has insisted on unsuitable people being engaged.

13 Supervise the First Course and Coach the Instructor

The first course using skills analysis techniques requires fairly close supervision from the training specialist responsible for its development. This does not mean that he has to be present all the time. He would be well advised, however, to appear at changeover periods scheduled in the timetable. This has the advantage not only of reminding the instructor it is time to move on to the next exercise, but also enables the training officer to assess progress during the important early stages. His periodical visits will grow less frequent as the course proceeds. At the end of each day, the training officer must find time to discuss with the instructor how the trainees have progressed. He will have doubts and queries, and these must be resolved as they arise. This personal coaching of the instructor is a necessary follow-up to his previous training before the course began.

14 Check Results and Follow up Trainees

The results of the first course must be carefully assessed. Were the preliminary exercises properly structured, or was too much or too little attempted at each stage? Was the build up to production speed correctly phased? The daily work sheets filled in by the learners act as a valuable *aide memoire* during the assessment. The follow-up of the trainees' progress in the production department is, of course, primarily the supervisor's responsibility. The training officer and instructor, however, should discuss progress with him, discuss any shortcomings revealed and the ways to overcome them.

15 Revise the Training Manual for Second Course

Undoubtedly, there will be a need to make revisions to the training manual for the second course. These should be discussed with the supervisor and the instructor, as both will have valuable contributions to make.

It can be seen that the training officer has a great deal to do if the first course using skills analysis is to be successful. He should be given time to carry out his programme and not be overloaded with a number of odd jobs. Once he has set up and administered one course, he will feel more confident and be able to handle more varied responsibilities.

Establishing the Right Climate for Training to Succeed

Training and development of people is a continuous process. The training committee is one way of ensuring that training effort is put into useful and economic channels, but in the long term it is the interest of the chief executive in the training officer's work which ensures continuing success. A wise chief executive will test 'user' reaction to the work of the training department at periodic intervals.

Are line managers still convinced that they are being provided with the service they require? If the answer is affirmative, the standards of performance of people within the company should steadily improve.

12. The future

In this final chapter, we take a look into the future, in the light of changes which are already becoming apparent today. It will not be enough for managers to provide effective training within their companies on the lines discussed in this book; they also bear responsibility for ensuring that their knowledge and attitude to training develops at the same rate as other changes which will affect them. Unless they are able to do this, training in their companies will fail to meet the real needs of the undertaking. Of the many changes which are taking place, we propose to discuss three which seem to us to be of far-reaching importance. They are: changes in technology, changes in the function of the working population, and changes in social environment at work.

Changes in Technology

A major aspect of technological change is likely to be the greater rate in developing completely new processes and industries. Much of the change which has taken place, so far, has been one of refinements and improvements in existing basic processes. In the future, whole new technologies will arise. This will mean that one of the more fascinating challenges that lie ahead will be concerned with the retraining of large numbers of workers over a relatively short period. Let us consider the type of training which will probably be required.

So far, one of the major effects of technological advance has been the removal of the need for people to use their muscles as motors. Machines can be built now that work faster, more accurately and consistently, more cheaply, and with less fatigue than human operators. The increasing use of machines and new materials has reduced the need for manual assembly. The result has been to place increasing emphasis on diagnostic and control skills at the expense of 'manual doing' skills, and this is a trend which is likely to continue. The efficiency of a plant will depend more on how quickly machine faults can be traced and rectified, rather than the speed at which manual operations take place. In fact, with highly automated or mechanized processes, the emphasis is shifting from 'how fast can the fault be diagnosed, rectified, and the machine restarted?' to 'how can we anticipate trouble before it arises?'. The need is not to restart machines quickly, but to prevent them from stopping. Therefore, the new skills will depend on the knowledge of systems (air, hydraulic, and electrical), and their operation on a machine. Coupled with a knowledge of basic operating systems will be the need to think logically or to use aids which will assist logical thinking.

Co-operation between production operators and maintenance staff assumes greater importance. The good production operator becomes the eyes and ears of the maintenance man. There are plenty of industrial examples of the importance of close working relationships between operators and maintenance staff.

In a highly mechanized foundry, frequent electrical breakdown occurred. The electricians who asked the operators for help in tracing faults were usually able to remedy them in a matter of minutes. Other electricians who regarded themselves as 'skilled men' with special expertise which must be closely guarded took hours to repair the same kind of fault, because they neither asked for nor received help from operators. The cost to a company of this kind of behaviour is enormous.

In a large machine shop, if one machine fails and the mechanic takes unduly long to repair it the production loss is limited to that machine. In highly mechanized machine shops, where one machine does the work of many, every minute of downtime is a matter of major concern.

The production operators and maintenance team must be able to communicate in the appropriate language. The maintenance man wants to know what happened prior to the stoppage and what the operator has done since it occurred. The operator wants to know what he can do to prevent a similar stoppage, or what to do if one should occur. As machines become increasingly automatic, the operator will have less to do. It seems logical to look forward to the eventual elimination of the distinction between operating and maintaining a machine; the same man will have to do both. Already, this trend is beginning as the distinction between different 'trades' in maintenance work is being blurred.

It is clear that training will have to develop at the same rate, or even slightly ahead, of technological change. The analysis of skills, 'how' to perform as well as 'what' to do, will be just as important as it is today—probably more so. The kinds of area that training will have to cover in the future are:

1 Knowledge of machine operating systems.
2 Knowledge of the whole machine process, not just one or two stages.
3 Knowledge of how each step in the process is achieved.
4 Knowledge of control information, how it is produced, in what form it is displayed, and how it can be used.
5 Fault-finding procedures and strategies for process production.
6 Skills of co-operation and teamwork.
7 Fault rectification procedures. Is it better to reset, repair, or to replace?
8 Techniques and use of preventive maintenance.
9 The reading of dials and displays.
10 Controlling factors in a process and their interaction.
11 The provision of effective operating manuals and other aids.

There is a paradox in all this. Although fewer people will require training, the cost per head of the training given is likely to increase sharply. Managers, when making investment decisions, will be wise to take into account not only the capital cost of the machine, but also the capital cost of setting up adequate training facilities for the people who are to be responsible for it. Although training costs per head will increase, the penalties for inadequate training and the rewards for doing training well, will become proportionately greater.

Another aspect of technological change is likely to be the greater emphasis on training white collar workers, such as draughtsmen and computer staff. In July 1967, the *Ministry of Labour Gazette*[1] records:

Whereas at one time the complexity of computers may have called for professional or graduate engineers for maintenance work, at the present state of development, the type of staff best suited for training are technicians with a good knowledge of electrical and mechanical engineering.

This downward trend in basic educational background required, before training can be given, is likely to continue for many occupations. However, the corollary is that the training staff must be of a higher standard. It will not be sufficient to let the 'intelligent university graduate' work it out for himself. More positive instruction is needed, and the basic principles of skills analysis still form the foundation on which a sound training programme can be built. Possibly the next big advance in non-supervisory training will be the reduction in traditional training times for white collar staff, of the same order as reductions have been made in training manual workers.

A third aspect of technological change is likely to be the greater rate of change in developing completely new processes and industries. Much of the change which has taken place has been one of refinements and improvements in existing basic processes. In the future, whole new technologies are likely to arise and the retraining of large numbers of workers over a relatively short period is one of the more fascinating challenges which lie ahead.

The Working Population

As manufacturing industry becomes increasingly automated, the function of the working population is gradually changing from manufacturing goods to providing services for the community. This is to be welcomed, for a rising standard of living and education tends to reduce the relative proportions of people who are content to do simple routine manual tasks. Fortunately, both these trends are gradual, but we need to pay increasing attention to training in service industries. A good start has been made, and in Great Britain training boards have been set up to foster training in some of the major service industries, such as Hotel and Catering and Retail Distribution. In these industries, training in social skills, and the desire to render a service, are as important as training in how to perform the service itself. The following story, no doubt apocryphal, illustrates the point well.

A BBC announcer was discussing with a porter on the railways how he was going to get to work on Christmas Day when the normal train service was to be curtailed drastically. The porter explained how important it was that railway staff should be able to spend Christmas at home with their families. 'Yes,' said the BBC announcer, 'but we have to go to work to provide the entertainment for you to have at home with your family.' 'That's quite

150

different,' said the porter. 'You see,' he explained helpfully, 'you're a public service.'

We can all cite examples of poor service in shops, hotels, transport undertakings, and so on, and we can all remember occasions when our wrath has been nullified by skilful handling of a complaint by a member of the organization's staff, or by a skilful handling of a potentially difficult situation by some other official. Here is another railway example—this time its authenticity is not in doubt.

Heavy snow fell overnight and disrupted London's Underground. At one station a big queue formed. At its head a porter controlled the crowd, explained what was happening, and the reasons for delay. As he let each batch of people on to the platform he reminded them not to push and rush as serious accidents occur that way. All went well and the next morning a notice was written on a blackboard. 'The staff of this station wish to thank passengers who co-operated so well with us during the difficult situation on Tuesday morning.'

There was nothing difficult in all this. The important element was a stationmaster who obviously had trained his staff well in how to handle the public. Much more work needs to be done to analyse the reasons for differences in performance between good and poor workers in service industries. Here again, it is a question of adapting analytical techniques and developing training schemes based on the analysis.

Often, poor service can be explained by lack of knowledge. The shop assistant who is not completely *au fait* with stock, the wine waiter who knows little about wine, the airline hostess who gives patently false reasons for delay. It is a natural human trait to try to cover up lack of knowledge by blustering or even abusive tactics. Much as managements deplore these results, and stress to their staff the importance of the philosophy 'the customer is always right', many customer complaints arise only as a symptom of a much deeper malaise. Managements should blame themselves, not their staffs. Has adequate training been given, or was the employee left largely to his own devices to pick up the knowledge required to give an adequate service? Experience is all very well, but, as in manufacturing industry, much of it can be analysed and taught. Are the procedures and the flow of communications in need of drastic overhaul?

The plane is late yet again. The reason given is 'technical trouble', a well-worn phrase that passengers have come to regard as an excuse for every failure. Yet, some passengers know that the traffic congestion was unavoidable due to a crash, which delayed the airport coach. Why weren't all the passengers told? And more important, why weren't the relatives and friends meeting the passengers at the destination also informed? It is unfair to blame the staff—though they get the blame. The real reason for failure lies in the lack of communication procedures, and training, prevailing in the airlines.

Another example may be given of a training investigation, based on analysis 'on the job', which revealed aspects of work organization in need of attention.

Although a ward sister in a hospital was in favour of her nurses chatting with patients, they never had time to sit down at the bedside. Nurses were in short supply and the work of the ward had to be done in time for doctors' visits, visiting hours, and other landmarks in a hospital day. Investigation showed that the ward routines, distribution of duties, and bed allocations could be altered in such a way that the same work could be done in less time. Nurses were encouraged to chat and sit with patients, a form of therapy likely to prove a great aid to more rapid recovery as many hospital patients know.

Though many people deplore the growth in numbers of civil servants and local government officials, it seems that the trend will continue as community life becomes more complex. Basic training in what to do is normally given. Training courses in procedures and basic knowledge requirements are reasonable, yet how little training is given in the application of that knowledge in the sense of it being a service to the community. Consider the reactions of the irate ratepayer trying to elicit an answer from a town hall, the harassed mother of six from a back street slum applying for National Assistance, or the man with a broken arm recently arrived at a poorly organized hospital casualty department. These are everyday examples and the officials concerned can give, no doubt, many reasons why each failure occurs. Yet, it is possible to cite examples of the helpful borough official, the sympathetic national assistance officer, the well-organized and efficient hospital casualty department. It is not sufficient to say that the differences lie in the personality and attitudes of the staff concerned. The differences, and the reasons for them, need analysing and recording at the place of work, where things happen. Revised procedures and revised training schemes can then be implemented to help raise standards. So far, only the surface of this problem has been touched—it remains one of the important training needs of the future.

Social Environment at Work

We hear a good deal today about industrial democracy. Why, the argument runs, should people have less control over their destinies in their working environment than in their lives as citizens? We believe this argument to be increasingly unreal. In fact, the worker has a good deal of control over the working environment. Much of this control is unfortunately exercised in a negative way, for example, by 'banking' work or restricting production. What is needed is to find a means of harnessing the deep knowledge which workers have of their jobs to positive production orientated objectives. This is a subject which cannot be dealt with fully in this book. We touch on it because we believe the training function has a contribution to make in this field.

In our experience, shop-floor relationships have always improved when a training analysis has been carried out. Sometimes, of course, this has been only a transitory improvement, but a gain has been made none the less. There is a simple and obvious explanation, namely that, sometimes for the first time, management has been seen to take a real and detailed interest in the skills and knowledge possessed by their workers. No worthwhile training analysis can take place unless the analyst is obviously interested in learning about both the successes and frustrations of shop-floor life. Often, particularly with maintenance workers, the people who learn most are those being analysed. Helping others to understand the details of one's own job gives a man a deeper understanding of what he is doing and leads to improvement. The old adage that the teacher learns most is very true. It is also a fact that as time passes all workers develop new and improved methods of doing a job, and this constantly developing expertise could be used in a positive way to improve productive efficiency.

There are, therefore, two aspects to the problem. The first, largely the field of the social scientists, is developing ways of convincing working groups that they have more to gain by using their expertise for increasing rather than restricting production. The second is to help people to understand and to improve the skills which they develop over the course of time. This is the province of the skills analyst. In the future, it is likely that he will not only assist in preparing training schemes for new employees, but will play his part in helping existing workers to understand and to improve their own skills. This is a vastly different matter from 'retraining', which tends to be a conscious management effort to improve performance, and is to this extent imposed from above. We are thinking more of the working group wanting to improve its own performance in line with management's overall objectives. This is by no means a Utopian concept, as a number of recent industrial experiments have shown.[2]

Before leaving the subject of the working environment, we must touch on the matter of fear of change. Changes take place all around us and in increasingly large numbers. Though most people say they welcome change, provided it is for the better, few of us really embrace the idea wholeheartedly—unless of course it is someone else, not ourselves, who is affected. In industry, the casualties from change are constantly with us. The redundant operator, the older worker forced to find a new job, the victim of a merger or closure. Increasingly today, people are being cushioned against the economic effects of change, redundancy payments, offers of alternative jobs, retraining, and similar measures. This is all very desirable but does little to strike at one of the major causes of fear of change—uncertainty regarding the future. Most people derive satisfaction from doing a job well, from being regarded as an experienced person in their chosen occupation. Imposed change, outside their control, threatens this security. If I am given a new job, how long will it be before I am regarded as a fully competent worker? Indeed, at my age, will I be able to master the new skills at all? It is certainly not enough to talk of training facilities being available. The training must be known to be adequate, speedy, and enable the displaced worker to regard himself as experienced in what he considers a reasonable time.

The point was illustrated many years ago in a cotton town in Lancashire. A mill had expanded and re-equipped with automatic looms but was experiencing difficulty in recruiting skilled weavers, although the pay and conditions were superior to the average in the district. A skills analysis based training centre was opened and school leavers trained in it on the automatic looms. It was also decided that any experienced weavers, who had no previous experi-

154

ence of the automatic looms, would be passed through the training centre before they took their positions in the mill. Each of these weavers would undergo a special training course based on her needs. At first no weavers applied, but after the first course of school leavers, one experienced weaver from another mill asked if she could undergo the same course. The firm's training policy was explained, i.e. all new weavers would be given training in the training centre. Within a fortnight the company had recruited sufficient experienced weavers for its needs.

The lesson is clear. Training for displaced persons must be known to be successful. It is equally true that if major changes are introduced into an existing department, they will be more readily accepted if adequate provision is made for retraining in the new skills required. This is another pointer for the future—an increasing emphasis on retraining to equip people to deal with change.

The Importance of the Learning Curve

Most people know intuitively that learning never stops. We improve the more we do a job. Until recently, the full implications of this fact have not been fully understood. We now know that the time to perform a task lessens, on average, by 20 per cent according to the nature of the task, for each doubling of the number of times we do it. Thus, the 1,000th attempt takes 20 per cent less time than the 500th, and the 2,000th attempt 20 per cent less time than the 1,000th. As jobs tend to alter with the passage of time, the ultimate in human performance is not reached. The implications of this for the training specialist will increase in importance.

First, he can no longer regard his standard training method as valid for as long as the job lasts. He will have to update his analysis periodically to take account of the improvements which have gradually been evolved by long-serving operators.

Secondly, he will be able to predict with some accuracy the number of attempts which will be required before the learner achieves the minimum acceptable performance.

In chapter 10, we referred to the training of welders for a new product. It was important that when the first component arrived for assembly that the welders could perform their tasks in a certain time. Each type of weld was mocked up at the training stage and the welders were given a predetermined number of attempts, in training, to ensure that they would be on the correct position on the 'learning curve' by the time production began.

The Carpet Industry Training Board is using the same principle to establish standard training times. A combination of skills analysis, learning curve principles, and knowledge of standard times for micromotions derived from predetermined motion time research work, enables the Board to make a reasonable deduction as to how long training times should be for an occupation, given that the training is soundly based.

So far, this work is only in its infancy, but clearly in the future training specialists will be able to make far more accurate predictions as to how long training for a task will take. This will have many implications for management; for example, when should recruitment take place? How much money should be allocated for training? How long will it before a new factory achieves optimum efficiency, and so on? Not least of the benefits will be the control of training staff to ensure they achieve the results predicted.

The Training Function in the Future

The central theme of this book has been that training is the responsibility of every manager and that good training pays. The real lesson is that it is not enough to state what has to be done, but that analysis has to be undertaken to help people understand how to achieve the what. This analysis nearly always reveals things which should be changed to enable the operator to perform really effectively. When developing a new process, for example, if constantly we ask not only what people have to do, but how, in detail, they are expected to do it, the answers to the question often lead to important and money-saving modifications of the process itself.

In the future, therefore, the training function is likely to assume greater significance in managerial practice. Training staff will need to be better qualified and trained to take their place as specialists who can make an important contribution to the wellbeing of their organization. Clearly, their links with the personnel function will be strengthened, for they are concerned with people at work, but above all the training specialist must develop the ability to talk knowledgeably about management matters to managers. Training will have arrived when its 'welfare' image has faded into oblivion. This is as true of the developing countries as it is in old-established industrial societies.

156

References

1 'The Occupational Effects of Technological Change': *Ministry of Labour Gazette*, July 1967, p. 540.
2 See notably *New Look Industrial Relations*: F. E. Oldfield, Mason Reed Limited, London.

Bibliography

Books

Training Managers: Michael Argyle and Trevor Smith. The Acton Society Trust, 1962.

Training the Adult Worker: Eunice Belbin. H.M.S.O. (Problems of Progress in Industry 15.)

Exploration in Management: Wilfred Brown. Heinemann, 1960.

'Evaluating the effectiveness of laboratory training in industry': P. C. Buchanan. A paper presented at an A.M.A. seminar on Applying the Behavioural Sciences to Management Skills, on February 24–26, 1964. New York, A.M.A., 1964.

How to Win Friends and Influence People. Dale Carnegie. The World's Work, 1953.

Group Dynamics: Research and Theory: Dorwin Cartwright and Alvin Zander (Eds.) Tavistock Publications, 1954.

Research in Relation to Operator Training: Hilary M. Clay. D.S.I.R., 1964.

Automation and Skill: E. R. F. W. Crossman. H.M.S.O., 1960. (Problems of Progress in Industry 9.)

Training made Easier: A Review of Four Recent Studies: Department of Scientific and Industrial Research. H.M.S.O., 1960. (Problems of Progress in Industry 6.)

Management of Training Programs: Frank A. DePhillips, *et al.* Richard D. Irwin, 1960.

159

Programmed Instruction for Industrial Training: Bernard Dodd. Heinemann, 1967.

The Effective Executive: Peter F. Drucker. Heinemann, 1967.

The Practice of Management: Peter F. Drucker. Heinemann, 1955.

The Industrial Supervisor. J. Munro Fraser and J. M. Bridges. Business Publications, 1964.

The Complete Plain Words: Sir Ernest Gowers. H.M.S.O., 1957.

New Developments in Training: Five Studies in the Efficient Communication of Skills. Frank A. Heller. Polytechnic Management Association, January 1959.

Theories of Learning: Ernest R. Hilgard. 2nd ed. Methuen, 1958.

Principles of Training: D. H. Holding. Pergamon Press, 1965.

Improving Business Results: J. W. Humble. McGraw-Hill, 1968.

Improving Management Performance: J. W. Humble. British Institute of Management, 1965.

Methods of Training Your Staff: Industrial Welfare Society. London, The Society, 1964. (Notes for Managers, No. 3.)

A 12-hour Training Programme for Supervisors: Industrial Welfare Society. The Society, 1965.

Costing the Training Function: Institute of Personnel Management. The Institute, 1965.

The Presentation of Technical Information: Reginald O. Kapp. Constable, 1958.

Training within the Organization: A Study of Company Policy and Procedures for the Systematic Training of Operators and Supervisors: David King. Tavistock Publications, 1964.

Vocational Training in View of Technological Change: S. D. M. King. Organisation for European Economic Co-operation, 1960. (E.P.A. Project, No. 418.)

Requirements for Basic and Professional Formal Education for Scientific Management: Harold Koontz, British Institute of Management, 1965.

An Approach to the Training and Development of Managers: Ministry of Labour. H.M.S.O., 1967.

Performance-oriented Training: Louis W. Lerda and Leslie W. Cross. Esso Standard Inc., 1961–62.

Training in Business and Industry: William McGehee and Paul A. Thayer. Wiley & Sons, 1961.

The Human Side of Enterprise: Douglas McGregor. McGraw-Hill, 1960.

Management Recruitment and Development: National Economic Development Council. H.M.S.O., 1965.

Developing Managerial Competence: Changing Concepts, Emerging Practices: National Industrial Conference Board. 1964. (Personnel Policy Study, No. 189.)

Primary Standard Data: Fred J. Neale. McGraw-Hill, 1967.

New Look Industrial Relations: F. E. Oldfield. Mason Reed, 1966.

Evaluation of Supervisory and Management Training Methods: Co-ordination of Research: Organization for Economic Co-operation and Development. O.E.C.D., 1963

Introduction to St Thomas Aquinas: J. Pieper. Faber, 1963.

The Academic Teaching of Management: Derek Pugh (Ed.). Basil Blackwell, 1966.

The Theory of Practice in Management: R. W. Revans. Macdonald, 1966.

A Time to Train. An Account of Experience gained by RTB at its Spencer Works. O. W. Reynolds and John Baker. Pergamon Press, 1966.

The Mensuration of Management: T. G. Rose. Manchester Municipal College of Technology, 1946. (Monograph, No. 3.)

Personal and Organizational Change through Group Methods: the Laboratory Approach: Edgar H. Schein and Warren G. Bennis. Wiley & Sons, 1965.

Retraining and Further Training: Dr. Gil Schonning. O.E.C.D., 1965.

Industrial Skills: W. Douglas Seymour. Pitman, 1966.

161

Industrial Training for Manual Operations: W. Douglas Seymour. Pitman, 1954.

Operator Training in Industry: W. Douglas Seymour. The Institute of Personnel Management, 1959.

Skills Analysis Training: W. Douglas Seymour. Pitman, 1968.

Mathematical Theory of Communication: Claude E. Shannon & Warren Weaver. University of Illinois Press, 1963 ed.

Selecting and Training the Training Officer: Nancy Taylor. Institute of Personnel Management, 1966.

Programmed Learning in Perspective: A Guide to Programme Writing: C. A. Thomas, *et al.* City Publicity Services Ltd. for Lamson Technical Products Ltd, 1963.

Evaluation of Training: K. E. Thurley. British Institute of Management, 1965.

Industrial Retraining Programs for Technological Change. A Study of the Performance of Older Workers: United States Department of Labor. United States Government Printing Office, 1963.

The Making of Scientific Management: L. Urwick and E. F. L. Brech. Vol. 1. Pitman, 1945.

Ageing and Human Skill: A Report centred on Work by the Nuffield Unit for Research into Problems of Ageing: A. T. Welford. O.U.P., for Nuffield Foundation, 1958.

The Training Revolution from Shop-floor to Board-room: John Wellens. Evans Brothers, 1963.

Apprenticeship in Europe: the Lesson for Britain: Gertrude Williams. Chapman & Hall, 1963.

Industrial Organization: Theory and Practice: Joan Woodward. O.U.P., 1965.

Experimental Psychology: Robert S. Woodworth and Harold Schlosberg. 3rd ed. Methuen & Co., 1954.

Articles

'Experiments on the Acquisition of Industrial Skills': W. Douglas Seymour. *Occupational Psychology*, April 1954, April 1955, April 1956, January 1959.

'Managing for Business Effectiveness': Peter F. Drucker. *Harvard Business Review*, May/June 1963.

'The Occupational Effects of Technological Change': *Ministry of Labour Gazette,* July 1967.

'Problems of Training the Immigrant Worker': Roy C. Williams. *Industrial Training International*, March 1968.

'Skills Analysis Training': John Ramsden. *Industrial Training International*, June 1966.

'A Standard Method of Costing the Training of Apprentices': BACIE *Journal*, September 1963.

'Training Workmen in Habits of Industry and Co-operation': H. L. Gantt. A paper from *Transactions of the American Society of Mechanical Engineers.* Vol. XXX. 1908.

Index

Index

167

Instructors—*cont.*
  coaching of, 145
  personal qualities, 80
  personal specification, 78
  rates of pay and status, 85
  selecting and training of, 144
  training of, 80, 81
Interviewing technique, 51

Johnson Radley Limited, 101, 109, 128

Kim's game, 34–6

Labour stability chart, 19, 20
Labour turnover, cost of, 137
  statistics, 19
Learning curve, 155
Learning graphs, 21, 22, 28, 136
Light assembly work, 127

Machine downtime, cost of, 137
Man/Machine Systems, 107, 122, 96
Management by objectives, 77, 108
Managers,
  relationship with, 84
  responsibility, 84
Mandleberg, J., 110
Manpower planning, 28
Method of learning,
  part, 36, 37
  whole, 36, 37
Methods Time Measurement, 49
Midvale Steel Company, 89

Off-the-job training, 54
On-the-job training, 54

Paine, Alan, Limited, 90
Perkins Engine Company, 91, 101, 109, 115
Personnel Management, 120
Physical skills analysis,
  identifying points of difficulty, 53
Pitfalls, 58
Programmed instruction, 33
Psychological and social factors in training, 56, 57

Quality control, 97
  quality control and training, case study, 97
  role of staff, 97
Quality specification, 25

Reads Limited, 99, 110, 140
Recruitment,
  difficulties in, 20
Resources for training, 30
Rest Pauses, 85
Retraining older workers, 56

Self-discipline, teaching of, 84
Simulators, 53
Skills analysis,
  definition of, 5, 37
Skills Analyst, 36
  place in organization, 119
Social environment, 153
Social geography, 56
Synthesis, 52
  definition of, 52

Taylor, F. W., 89
Technology, changes in, 74, 147–50
Trainees, 82–4
  follow-up, 93
  payment of, 86
  a personal specification of, 83, 84
  selection of, 82, 83
Training, 136
  assembly lines, 127
  automated industry, 96, 107, 122, 148
  budgets, 112
  changes in the product, 29
  cost control statements, 113
  current cost of, 22
  establishing a standard method for training purposes, 143
  facilities, 111
  national and cultural factors, 58
  needs for new factories, 29
  organization, 93
  plans, 110
  preliminary syllabus, 140
  resources, 110

Training—*cont.*
service industries, 150–2
small numbers of trainees, 126, 127
social skills, 150
syllabus, 140, 142
where to start deciding, 138
white collar workers, 149
Training approach for process industry, 74
Training centre, use for special production work, 125
Training for changes in the product, 29
Training Committees, 100, 139
case study, 101
Training course,
time needed for preparation of, 25
preparation and running, 142–5
Training elements, 37
Training expenditure, 91
Training function, its place in the organization, 118
Training of immigrants, 58
Training instructor,
place in the organization, 118
Training manager, 104
five ingredients for a successful training manager, 107
place in the organization, 119–21
Training needs analysis, 16, 109, 136
accident rates, 24
current cost of training, 22
general production background, 24
information required, 18

the labour force, 16
length of present training, 21
machine utilization, 24
present learning difficulties, 25
present performance of operators, 21
present training arrangements, 23
quality information, 25
range of work, 16
recruitment and selection arrangements, 24
Training needs assessment, 26
Training officers, 72–7
and size of company, 72
and new machinery, 123
as managers, 73
knowledge and skills which should be possessed by, 73
key result areas of training officer's job, 76
performance standards for, 76
selection of, 72
training of, 73–7
Training policy, 11, 91
development of, case study, 91
Training programmes,
design of, case study, 61
design of, 52
'exporting', 58
Training staff, 4
Training technology, 53

Universal products, 7
Urwick Management Centre, 63

Wedgwoods, 119
Work Study Department, 95
Working groups, 100

Printed in Great Britain by
Cox & Wyman Ltd., London, Fakenham and Reading